MW01592716

87 MARSHALL STREET

CREATION, DISRUPTION,
AND RENEWAL IN THE
NORTHERN BERKSHIRES

JOHN L. SPRAGUE

Copyright © 2016 by John Sprague
ISBN-10:0-9829914-9-5
ISBN-13:978-0-9829914-9-7
Printed in Canada

CONTENTS

ARNOLD PRINTWORKS
C. 1881

FOREWORD

The title of this intriguing book refers to a group of structures situated at the very heart of North Adams, Massachusetts, a small, postindustrial city nestled in a river valley overshadowed by the Berkshire mountains to the east and the Taconic Range to the west. Today, that sprawling complex of nineteenth-century factory buildings houses the celebrated Massachusetts Museum of Contemporary Art and is listed on the National Register of Historic Places. Widely admired both at home and abroad for the enterprising, avant-garde nature of its rotating exhibitions, the museum houses an extensive collection of exquisite Sol LeWitt renditions, as well as vast and brooding Anselm Kiefer paintings and, appropriately enough, a monumental sculpture by the latter's fellow countryman and colleague, Joseph Beuys. All of this is well known, and the residents of North Adams take justifiable pride in their city's serving as host to a museum of international reputation.

Less well known, at least to the world at large, is the fact that these grand old industrial buildings were, for the better part of a century, home to two successive manufacturing enterprises of great ambition and scope. In their day, both stood like colossi dominating their particular niches in what were brutally competitive global markets. By the start of the twentieth century, the first of those enterprises, Arnold Print Works, had become one of the world's largest textile printing corporations. After its mid-century failure and decline into ultimate bankruptcy, its successor tenant at the Marshall Street complex, the Sprague Electric Company, succeeded in the teeth of cut-throat global technological and marketing competition in becoming one of the world's largest electronic component manufacturers. In each case, this was unquestionably a somewhat extraordinary outcome. In that of Sprague, in particular, it was an outcome no less dramatic than extraordinary, and one that, as subsequent events were to prove, could easily be imperiled.

War and peace, technology and timing, feast and famine—the story of Sprague Electric is a gripping one. It is marked by not only the skillful surfing of oceanic business cycles, but also a stomach-churning willingness to make high-risk strategic decisions. Such skill and willingness were necessary if the company was to survive and prosper in an industry characterized by razor-thin profit margins and relentless global technological competition. It is a story that has long needed to be told, and who better equipped to tell it—by background, experience, talent, and training—than John Sprague himself?

Raised in Williamstown, John Sprague has extended family roots in the northern Berkshires, an area where he has spent most of his life and to which he is deeply attached. After Navy service and PhD research at Stanford University, he returned to Massachusetts in 1959 to join the family enterprise, which was closing in on its period of greatest prominence. Semiconductors were his area of specialty and, after working in research and development in North Adams, he moved on to head up the Sprague Semiconductor Group in Worcester, Massachusetts. Later, at a time when the company was finding itself condemned to tacking laboriously in the teeth of increasingly severe global headwinds, he returned to North Adams to take on challenging roles at Sprague Electric Company, first as president and chief operating officer, and then as chief executive officer. As a result, he carries in his very bones the dramatic story of the company's rise and fall; the daunting challenges it encountered in its latter years remain deeply etched in his consciousness. In one way or another, after all, his own life has been intertwined with the life of the company, since its glory days in the early 1960s. He was still in Worcester during the debilitating strike at Sprague's North Adams hub in 1970, the fallout from which has endured to the present day; he was serving in the executive trenches during the later downturn in the company's fortunes and its acquisition, successively, by General Cable and Penn Central in 1976 and 1981. His years as CEO postdated the concomitant passage out of the hands of the Sprague family and its control over its ultimate destiny.

Scar tissue from this bruising, roller-coaster sequence of events remains well distributed among former employers, employees, and local government officials alike, and there is much that remains unrecognized or controverted about the trials and tribulations of the company's final years. John Sprague does not flinch from addressing the neuralgic issues involved. He does so without any extended exercise in self-justification and with a refreshing openness to criticism. In so doing, he brings to the task the characteristic objectivity, forthrightness, and honesty that those who know him well have long since come to admire in him…and the story he tells is a compelling one.

Francis Oakley
President Emeritus
Williams College
Williamstown, Massachusetts

PREFACE

After spending much of the previous ten years involved in two different biographies of my paternal grandfather—electrical inventor Frank J. Sprague—I set out to write a history of the Sprague Electric Company, where I worked from 1959 until 1987. I grew up in Williamstown, Massachusetts, with detours along the way in Concord, Massachusetts (Middlesex School), Princeton University, the US Navy, and Stanford University. My wife and I were married in 1952, and although we have always thought of Williamstown as our home, we moved a lot, settling at different times in Norfolk, Virginia; Burlingame and Palo Alto, California; Holden and Lincoln, Massachusetts; and Stamford, Connecticut. Each time we came home I was struck by the sheer beauty of the Berkshires, and we finally returned to the area for good in 1995. We live on the east side of the Taconic Range, and at times it seems like a game preserve: deer abound, as do black bear (occasionally on our deck), fox, raccoon, porcupine, mink, coyote, fisher, and even a resident bobcat.

When I started to work on the Sprague story, I spent time at the Massachusetts Museum of Contemporary Art (MASS MoCA) complex at 87 Marshall Street, the address in North Adams that was once the headquarters of Sprague Electric. Most of the former manufacturing spaces are now galleries, but there are signs of the past everywhere, including one of my old offices. I began to

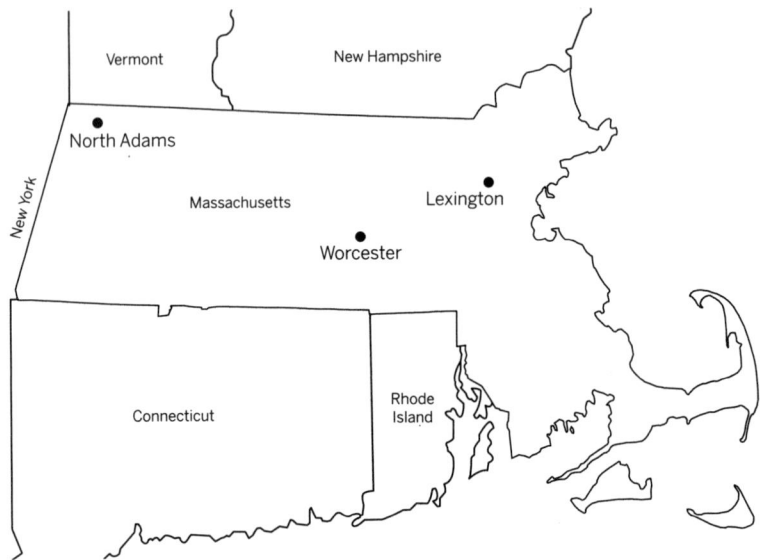

Map of the state of Massachusetts and surrounding states

see there was a bigger story enfolding that just that of the company I knew so well. How did Sprague Electric and Arnold Print Works, its predecessor on the site, become so successful while headquartered in such a seemingly isolated location? Although employee quality of life could certainly have been a contributing factor in this industrial success, there had to be more involved than just the wild beauty of the northern Berkshires.

I also recognized that—as is true throughout the Berkshires, in much of the Northeast, and in other parts of the United States— the local economy was suffering, with most of the manufacturing jobs that once fueled growth now gone. Great mills stand empty and abandoned, have been turned into condominiums, or are home to collections of small businesses. Instead of growing, populations are declining, and many cities and towns are becoming retirement communities, with the arts and tourism perhaps the new growth engine. As our country transitions from an industrial to postindustrial economy, despite the political rhetoric, not just North Adams but our entire society faces an uncertain future.

The story of Sprague Electric and the former mill town surrounding it offers a fascinating window into the past, present, and even future of our society. Before the Europeans came, indigenous tribes congregated in the area. Fur traders arrived, first bartering with and then fighting the native land-holders—and eventually each other. Crude dams and primitive mills appeared, clinging precariously to the shores of the raging north and south branches of the Hoosic River that converge at 87 Marshall Street. The hardiest survived and, as industry slowly began to flourish, textile, shoe, and other factories replaced the earlier structures, initially using water power to drive their equipment. As different immigrant groups populated the workforce, the surrounding community evolved into a collection of ethnic villages.

In the middle 1800s, Arnold Print Works began to construct a massive complex of some twenty-six buildings, most of which still stand today at 87 Marshall Street, and by 1900 Arnold had become one of the world's leading textile printing corporations. Hard times ensued, the result of an unfortunate management gamble on cotton futures and increasingly effective competition from southern-based factories. Consequently, Arnold Town, as some called North Adams during the Arnold ascendency, began its transition to Sprague Town, after a brash young electronics firm that moved from Quincy, Massachusetts, to North Adams at the beginning of the Great Depression.

Sprague Electric was located first on Beaver Street, next purchased a vacant mill on Brown Street, and during World War II replaced now-bankrupt Arnold Print Works as the owner and tenant of 87 Marshall Street. Fueled first by the War, then the Cold War and space age that followed, and finally by the surging computer industry, Sprague grew to be one of the world's leading electronic component manufacturers. At its peak in the 1980s, Sprague Electric's revenues exceeded $500 million, and the company employed over twelve thousand in some twenty-four locations around the world. Nonetheless, difficulties had begun to surface twenty years earlier, starting with growing labor problems in North Adams, and eventually questionable strategic decisions and increasingly strong Asian competition brought things to a head.

Between 1976 and 1984, Sprague was acquired twice, and its headquarters moved out of North Adams; by 1992 all its divisions had been sold off, and Sprague Electric had disappeared as an entity. Today, the $20 billion global capacitor market is dominated by Japanese corporations, with mainland China lurking in the wings. Sprague Electric no longer exists, but the story of its sixty-four-year life span describes a remarkable journey, full of highs and lows, and essential contributions to technology and the economy, both local and national. For the fifty-five years it was based in North Adams, Sprague played a huge role in the life of the city.

Completing the postindustrial transition, the current tenant of 87 Marshall Street, MASS MoCA, is one of the world's largest contemporary art museums. Where thousands of workers once operated complex machinery for printing cloth and later oversaw sophisticated electronic component assembly equipment, now visitors wander at leisure through galleries and studios, enjoying the visual and performing arts on display in a new world dominated not by manufacturing, but by arts and tourism. Even though MASS MoCA has saved North Adams from economic oblivion, transition has been difficult for the city and its people, because there are simply not enough jobs. While there are no easy answers to this problem, I conclude with a discussion of potential new business directions to complement the current emphasis on the arts, the creative economy, and tourism.

The heart of this book is an attempt to tell the Sprague Electric story clearly and honestly, from the point of view of one who personally lived that story and knows it intimately from the technical and management sides. But the history of 87 Marshall Street is also the fascinating story of a hard-working Massachusetts community and its resilient residents.

John L. Sprague

PROLOGUE

A VISIT TO MASS MOCA

Several years ago, on a crisp October day, I found myself with time to spare as I returned home to Williamstown from a business trip to Boston. On the spur of the moment, I took a nostalgic detour to North Adams, a historic mill town in the northern Berkshire hills, to visit MASS MoCA. I had worked in the complex that now houses the museum for many years, when the remarkable buildings were the headquarters of Sprague Electric Company.

In the fall, the view from the western summit of the Mohawk Trail is breathtaking, punctuated by the vibrant scarlet hues of the sugar maples. Directly below, North Adams is laid out in a mostly north-south direction. Further west, the valley narrows, bordered on the north side by Pine Cobble Mountain and on the south by Mount Williams and then Mount Greylock, the highest mountain in the state.

Across the valley, at the base of Mount Williams, sits a small airport that offers scenic airplane rides over the area, while in the distance the Taconic Range, fronted by Williamstown, bars the entrance to nearby New York State; immediately to the north lie Vermont and eventually Canada. Some twenty miles south are Pittsfield and the other smaller communities that make up southern Berkshire County. This small piece of paradise is tucked in the very northwest corner of Massachusetts and appears isolated

MASS MoCA parking lot.
Photo: Zoran Orlic

from the rest of the world, as it actually was before the mid-1880s opening of the Hoosac Railroad Tunnel that now cuts through the Hoosac Range.

That day I began the steep descent toward the valley, safely negotiating the famous Hairpin Turn, and was soon passing a number of old mill buildings that have been put to new uses as I entered the outskirts of North Adams. Before long 87 Marshall Street, the immense MASS MoCA compound, loomed directly ahead.

On one side of Marshall Street stood a flat-roofed, two-story tan brick building that, although of a much newer vintage, remained a modest reminder of a past I knew well: the former home of

Don Gummer sculpture, *Primary Separation*, at former Sprague Electric Research Center. Photo: Elizabeth Berg

Sprague Research. I occupied an office in the building from 1962 until 1968. Now a recent MASS MoCA installation—a huge rock separated cleanly into two sections and suspended from a complex of eight vertical metal columns and heavy cables, Don Gummer, *1969/2005*, Polich Art Works, NY—hung before it.

Across the road, the names of MASS MoCA's current exhibitions were posted under the large museum sign on the old factory wall: *Anselm Kiefer*; *Eastern Standard: Western Artists in China*; *Badlands*; *Music, Dance, Theater, Film*; and the main installation, *Jenny Holzer: Projections*. Yet one of the aged stone pillars at what had been the main entrance to Sprague Electric boasted a plaque honoring a much older era:

MASS MoCA main entrance and *Tree Logic*
Photo: Zoran Orlic

The Johnson Grays
The First Volunteer Company
From North Adams
In The Civil War
Camped On These Grounds
And In June 1861
Became Co B 10th Regiment
Massachusetts Volunteer Infantry
This Tablet Erected By
C D Sanford Womans Relief Corps
June 1909

Entering the museum, I passed Natalie Jeremijenko's *Tree Logic* (1999), featuring six trees hanging upside down from their root balls, their limbs and trunks desperately twisting to seek the sky above, followed by another sign held over from the Sprague Electric industrial period:

Tantalum
Purchasing
Shipping
QAR
N. A. Purchasing

In the lobby, the ticket counter was crafted from a large metal I-beam removed from one of the buildings during the renovation process; directly behind it hung a small, square, blue and white clock with the Sprague logo, The Mark of Reliability. A wall plaque gave a brief history of this multi-story building:

Building 10
Arnold Print Works, which used Building 10 for printing designs on cotton cloth, modified and added to existing structures as its business expanded rapidly in the last quarter of the 19th century.

I later learned that when Arnold occupied the building, it was here that workers fed huge rolls of unfinished cotton cloth into massive multi-color machines that imprinted the designs using a series of rollers. As I remember it, during the tenancy of Sprague Electric Company, Building 10 housed an employee cafeteria, laboratories, and offices.

Looking outside, I was once more reminded of the vastness of the facility, seeing the numerous overhead bridges and driveways interconnecting the many buildings, while another plaque described the architectural changes made to create the current structure:

Building 11
Arnold Print Works used Building 11 as its "color shop," the place where the pigments for printing cotton textiles were mixed. Later it functioned as the shipping and receiving department for the Sprague Electric Company. The building started as a single brick building but today consists of five combined structures, some of which have been altered considerably.

In the first-floor galleries, I viewed *Badlands: New Horizons in Landscape*, featuring the work of some twenty artists and contributors, including Mary Temple's deceptively simple *Northeast Corner, Southwest Light*, a painting that gave the shadowy impression of light from a window, with background foliage, barely visible on two walls and the floor.

Straight ahead, in the stunning three-story space known as the Tall Gallery, I could see the new and unusual inverted truss system supporting the roof, as it does throughout much of the renovated space. On the far wall was Alexis Rockman's huge, seven-panel *South*, a beautiful Antarctic landscape primarily in brilliant blues and whites, with a shoreline bordering open water filled with icebergs and underwater scenery. Among the other works in the gallery, I was particularly struck by Jennifer Steinkamp's mesmerizing *Mike Kelley*, a huge holographic tree that continuously moved, changing both shape and color. Seated on the bench in front of the piece, I found the effect hypnotic.

Strolling through the exhibitions, I entered the W.L.S. Spencer Gallery where I was fascinated by three wind turbine "studies" by Joseph Smolinski: a model of a station for charging electric cars, a flat panel display with continually changing digitally generated scenes involving wind turbines, and a painting titled *Spinning Trees for Spent Oil*. In another part of the gallery, an audiovisual presentation by Jane D. Marsching and Terreform discussed the projected impact of global warming on land masses. This disturbing work showed major coastal cities worldwide disappearing beneath rising oceans.

In the final part of the gallery, overlooking the river and River Street towards Porches inn, five Vaughn Bell Personal Home Biospheres were suspended from the ceiling, each with a hole to insert one's head. Once "inside," for the briefest of times I was no longer in the museum but lost in some primitive rain forest.

Several of the main exhibitions were located on the second floor, including *Narrow are the Vessels* and other work by Anselm Kiefer. My wife and I first encountered Kiefer several years ago at Le Petit Palais in Paris, which, despite its name, is a huge space filled with massive sculptures and paintings that deplore war and destruction. Moving on to the Fulkerson Family Gallery, I found one of MASS MoCA's earliest installations, Joseph Beuys's large sculpture *Lightning with Stag in its Glare*—which had been hauled by crane into the gallery—on long-term loan from the Philadelphia Museum of Art.

Reversing direction and walking west brought me to the museum's largest and best-known gallery: Building 5. Created by removing the numerous walls and the ceiling that previously enclosed the Sprague Electric manufacturing spaces, it is two stories high, the length of a football field, and perhaps the largest of its kind in the world. The first work to be shown in this gallery was Robert Rauschenberg's mammoth *The 1/4 Mile or 2 Furlong Piece*.

Started by the artist in 1981 and still unfinished at the time of his death in May 2008, the colorful multimedia work stretched the full length of two 300-foot walls, with individual pieces strategically placed on the gallery floor. This work surrounded the invited guests at the opening gala in May 1999 as they sat at round dinner tables, seemingly immersed in the artwork.

On this visit, the giant space was filled with thirteen bus-sized inflated bags interconnected by tubular ducts, Tim Hawkinson's *Überorgan*. Its control mechanism was a 200-foot-long roll of Mylar that operated much like a player piano. It sounded as if one were inside a massive foghorn gone berserk, and visitors loved it.

As I wandered towards the exit, beautiful bells began to ring. A glass door revealed a stairway leading up to the bell tower, with another historical plaque that briefly described how the clock tower had been previously used: first by Arnold Print Works, which built it, and then by Sprague Electric Company. I knew it well, since in the 1977 General Cable Annual Report (General Cable acquired Sprague Electric in 1976) there was a photograph of then Sprague Electric chief executive officer Neal Welch and me, the company president, at the base of the tower. Back then the bells were real, but now, as the plaque detailed, they toll electronically in precise response to current light conditions, programmed by Christina Kubisch, a classically trained musician and professor of experimental art.

A lot of history has been written in this tiny corner of the world. Yet, driving home to Williamstown, I recognized that, except for the chronicles of Sprague Electric Company in North Adams, I knew very little about this extraordinary place where I had both lived and worked for much of my life. The venerable walls of 87

Marshall Street had been a witness to that history, and I decided that the time had come to broaden my horizons and tell their story…

CHAPTER ONE

IN THE BEGINNING

GEOGRAPHY

—

The topography of the protected valley where North Adams now sits, as well as the rivers that ultimately determined how the land would be used, were formed by a very slow geological process lasting over hundreds of millions of years. The gentle mountains and valleys we now see resulted from the weathering of three distinct forms of bedrock that were originally formed in horizontal layers, as the ancient Proto-Atlantic Ocean that covered the area receded and then crumpled into folds due to plate collision.

Some five hundred million years ago, this area was part of an ancient landmass called Laurentia. The raw materials that with time, extreme temperature, and pressure eventually became today's quartzite, marble, and slate, were all in place, in the form of sandy beaches on the edge of the ocean, in shallow water mineral deposits of limestone and dolomite, and as deep water muds. Laurentia and the Shelburne Falls volcanic chain collided 485 to 440 million years ago, creating a massive mountain chain running in a north-south direction. Looking at today's gentle remnants of this ancient collision, such as the Taconic Range that straddles the western Massachusetts border with New York State, it is hard to imagine that at one time these gentle hills were as rugged as today's Himalayas, which were formed much more recently when the Indian and Asian continents collided.

The slow erosion process began when cyclonic winds and water started to wear down the towering peaks. However, the different types of bedrock have very different weathering rates. For example, quartzite is extremely hard and chemically resistant. Therefore the tops of local ridges which are clad with this material, such as Pine Cobble and Stone Hill in Williamstown, Massachusetts, and the adjacent Dome, in Vermont, have been slow to weather. On the other hand, marble, which was created from limestone and dolomite deposited over much of the area, is extremely soft and also deteriorates chemically in our wet climate. Today it lies largely under the deep valleys where the rivers run. The third type of rock, which was formed from the deep sea muds and whose common forms are slate, phyllite, and schist, is quite chemically resistant and makes up a large part of the Taconic, Greylock, and Hoosac Ranges. Mount Greylock is interesting since it also contains a large body of very pure calcite marble at the lower level of its eastern side—now the Specialty Minerals quarry in Adams, Massachusetts.

Some eighteen thousand years ago, this entire area was covered by a continental ice sheet at least three thousand feet in thickness. All the peaks were hidden, including Greylock, and as the ice moved slowly southeast it shaped but didn't change the basic topography. The previous global warming cycle, which began around fifteen thousand years ago, caused the ice sheet to melt. Blocked to the west, south, and east by mountain ranges and to the north by an ice dam created by the receding ice, 450-foot-deep Lake Bascom was formed. As the dam slowly drained, mountain streams deposited their sediment, forming deltas in the lake at different levels. Coarser material was deposited close to the shoreline, while fine sediment and clay ended up in the deepest part of the lake. Today these are the valleys that formed after the dam finally broke and the lake drained through the Hoosac Valley into the Hudson River. This process continued for several hundred years, forming three distinct beach and delta levels.

As one might expect, the nature of these sedimentary deposits has directly affected land use. For example, the clay-rich soil of the lowest valleys is poor for crops, so farmers have tended to choose the sandy and better-drained soils along the former shorelines. Many of the deltas and former beaches now serve as commercial sources of sand and gravel. These, as well as other permeable deposits along the valley margins, also serve to collect rainfall and snowmelt from the higher elevations and channel the water to the lowest parts of the valley, where they have become an excellent source of well water protected beneath hundreds of feet of impermeable glacial lake clays.[1] With the basic topography in place, the region was a spectacularly beautiful wilderness, ready to be discovered, then explored, tamed, and finally settled.

FIRST SETTLERS

—

While the earliest human remains found in New England date back some twelve thousand years, debate continues today about when and how the first humans arrived in the Americas. In one controversial proposal, they came from Europe some thirteen thousand years ago, crossing the North Atlantic on glacial ice floes.[2] However, most theories have them crossing from northeast

---

1   Reinhard A. Wobus, The Geology of Williamstown: Historical and Practical Perspectives (Professor of Geology, Williams College), undated; Wobus to the author, August 14, 2011.

2   "Solutrean Hypothesis," http://en.wikipedia.org/wiki/Solutrean_hypothesis

Asia to Alaska more than fifteen thousand years ago on a land bridge (Beringia) that existed between the two continents at the end of the last ice age. Suggested routes for exploration of the Americas include small boats along the west coast and different dry-land routes below the receding ice sheets.[3] Therefore, as we follow the European settlement of North America, it must be remembered that Native Americans began to populate and form increasingly sophisticated societies more than ten thousand years before the white people arrived and started to occupy and seize the land from its original occupants.[4]

As far back as the 1400s, fur traders, primarily from the Netherlands, France, and England, came to the Americas and established a brisk bartering business with the Natives, offering metal goods, ornaments, glass, and later firearms and liquor, for a variety of local goods—especially animal pelts, of which beaver was the most prized because of its use in stylish felt hats. In general, early relations were cordial, although this began to change as the beaver population dropped precipitously and colonization began, following the 1620 landing of the Pilgrims at Plymouth.[5] Cordial or not, the early traders carried something else with them that, between 1600 and 1700, caused the Native population in New England to drop from seventy thousand to less than twelve thousand. The Old World disease, smallpox, to which the local people had no resistance, wiped out entire villages, causing far more

---

3 Heather Pringle, "The First Americans," Scientific American, November 2011, p. 36.

4 A. G. Bain, L. Manring, and B. Matthews, "Native Peoples of New England," (http://memorialhall.mass.edu/classroom/curriculum_6th/lesson2/)

5 William Cronon, Changes in the Land (New York: Hill and Wang, a Division of Farrar, Straus, and Giroux, 1983), p. 20.

damage than the wars that eventually followed.[6]

However, it was their completely different views of land owner-ship that created the greatest tension between the English settlers and the Native Americans. To the English, land, and everything on it, was the property of the owner. Houses were especially prized, and the social position of the owner was often determined by the nature of his home and personal property. The indigenous people owned little in the way of personal goods and were mo-bile, continually moving around the general area they occupied as food availability changed with the seasons and they searched for more fertile land to cultivate when soil became sterile. As animal pelts grew ever scarcer, in order to continue trading they were forced to "sell" their land to the settlers. To the Natives this meant allowing the settlers to share use of the land. To the English, it was now theirs.[7]

In addition, the English tended to despise the Natives, consid-ering them to be lazy heathen savages and homeless wanderers, with no property rights to the land on which they "wandered." Therefore the British Crown felt it had every right to empower the Massachusetts Bay Colony to create settlements wherever they wished.[8] Clearly, something had to give in this increasingly difficult situation.

---

6 Cronon, p. 82

7 Cronon, p. 65.

8 Cronon, p. 69.

PEACE ENDS

—

As the Native American population continued to die from diseases they couldn't control, and the English seized their lands, all civility disappeared for good when in 1675 Metacom, the Sachem or leader of the Wampanoags in eastern Massachusetts, attacked Swansea, near today's Springfield, and King Philip's War began. Although lasting little over a year, the war saw atrocities on both sides. For a while it looked as if the English might be pushed back into the sea, and, before Metacom was finally captured and executed in mid-1676, more than half of New England's towns had been attacked, thousands had died on both sides, and settlement of the western part of Massachusetts was delayed another fifty years.[9] In return, Native culture in southeastern New England had been destroyed, and many survivors were sold into slavery or servitude.

To the west in the Hudson River Valley, the most powerful indigenous confederation was that of the Iroquois or "Five Nations," which may have existed as far back as the twelfth century. Led by the powerful Mohawks, the other tribes were the Oneida, Onondaga, Cayuga, and Seneca (all familiar names today). Later they were joined by the Tuscarora to form the Six Nations Confederacy. Primarily located on the western side of the Hudson River, in what we now call upstate New York, they fought with neighboring tribes such as the Mohicans, eventually forcing them to the eastern side of the Hudson.

The early settlers from European nations came for varying

---

9   Walter Giersback, "America's Most Devastating Conflict," July 2004, www.militaryhistory.com

reasons. The Dutch pioneered the Hudson Valley after it was explored in 1606 by English navigator Henry Hudson on the Half Moon, while he was employed by the Dutch East India Company. Their primary interest was to establish an early trading presence, but they were also able to form reasonably friendly relations with the Iroquois, and founded Fort Orange (Albany) in 1624. A year later they founded New Amsterdam (New York City) as a major trading center, only to lose it in 1664 following a surprise attack by the English. After ten years of warfare between the two nations, in 1674 the Dutch ceded all of their Northeast territory to the English in the Treaty of Westminster.

In 1608 the French founded Quebec in the St. Lawrence Valley. While their prime interest was trade, their seemingly endless worldwide conflict with the English was another driving force.

For the English, although trade was also a consideration, in southeastern New England their driving ambition was colonization of the New World. However, before settlement could really proceed, even with the successful conclusion of King Philip's War there were four successive European conflicts to resolve, primarily with the French, and each with a New World component.

In 1689 King William's War[10] began when William III of England allied himself with several European states to oppose French worldwide expansion. In North America, the key issue was control of the fur trade. The Iroquois joined the English, and battles with the French were fought up and down the length of the Hudson Valley, as well as in Nova Scotia and New England, before peace was declared in 1697 in the Treaty of Ryswick. This

---

10   "King William's War," www.u-s-history.com and http://en.wikipedia.org/wiki/King_William's_War

was a short-lived peace, since nothing had really been resolved.

A conflict over succession to the Spanish throne, known as Queen Anne's War,[11] quickly spread to the New World in 1702. There were attacks across the Northeast by the French and their Algonquian allies, including an especially ferocious assault in February 1704 against Deerfield, Massachusetts, during which fifty-six settlers were massacred and one hundred driven on foot through heavy snows to Canada. The war ended in 1713 with the Treaty of Utrecht, which left still-inexact boundaries for parts of the disputed territory.

European hostilities renewed in 1740 as the English battled France, Prussia, and Spain over succession following the death of the Holy Roman Emperor, Charles VI. The North America component was known as King George's War,[12] where the French attacked Canso, Nova Scotia, and battles raged across Maine and the Hudson River Valley. Many died, but again neither side emerged victorious following the shaky 1748 Treaty of Aix-la-Chapelle.

These prior conflicts were really skirmishes leading up to the worldwide conflict known as the Seven Years' War, which lasted from 1756 to 1763, and was referred to in North America as the French and Indian War.[13] When it was over, not only was France no longer an important colonial power in North America but, with the Native presence largely dissipated, the rapid settlement

---

11   "Queen Anne's War," http://en.wikipedia.org/wiki/Queen_Anne's_War

12   "King George's War," www.u-s-history.com

13   "The French and Indian War," www.u-s-history.com, and World Book 2004 (Chicago, IL: World Book, Inc.).

1933 replica of Fort Massachusetts
Image courtesy of North Adams Historical Society

of western New England began. Yet wars create strange bedfellows; in an ironic twist of fate, only some twenty years after the start of this war, France would ally with the colonists to overthrow the English. Conveniently forgotten was the fact that in earlier conflicts the French had promised bounties to their tribal allies for the scalps of all the settlers, including those of women and children.[14]

The European phase of the Seven Years' War began when Frederick the Great of Prussia invaded Saxony, and initially pitted Prussia and Britain against an alliance that included Austria,

---

14   www.berkshireweb.com/mohawktrail/ftmass

France, Russia, Sweden, and Saxony. Other nations were drawn in, and soon all the major European powers were involved. It is estimated that the related worldwide loss of life exceeded one million people. In anticipation of such a conflict, the Massachusetts colonists had been making preparations for more than ten years, laying the groundwork in the Berkshires for what would become Williamstown, Adams, and North Adams.

In an attempt to protect the widely scattered settlements in the western end of Massachusetts from marauding Natives (overlooking, of course, the fact that this was really still their land), in 1744 the Massachusetts General Court had ordered the construction and garrisoning of a string of forts. One of these was Fort Massachusetts, built in 1745. Captain Ephraim Williams Jr., a member of the powerful Williams family that played such an important role in the settlement of western Massachusetts, was placed in command of the fort, as well as eleven others scattered throughout the region. From a military standpoint it was a poor location. The first Fort Massachusetts was a modest structure of several blockhouses surrounded by a log stockade, located in an open field, and vulnerable to sharpshooters on the surrounding high ground. It garrisoned only fifty men, and often many of these were away, gathering supplies or on scouting missions. In 1746 an estimated five hundred French and Native Americans attacked and, easily overcoming the small garrison of only twenty-two, burned it to the ground. Captain Williams was absent at the time. The few survivors were sent to Canada, where records indicate that they were humanely treated. A much more substantial fort was rebuilt the following winter, and it successfully withstood periodic further attacks and remained standing many years after the war ended. Now a Colonel, Ephraim Williams Jr. was killed in September 1755 while leading a regiment against the French entrenched near Crown Point. However, the legacy of

Colonel Williams and his Fort Massachusetts garrison runs much deeper. His will left the bulk of his estate to the formation of a free school (which became Williams College in 1793) in West Township (renamed Williams Town in 1765, as requested in the will), and many from the garrison were among the earliest settlers in the area after the war ended.[15]

With a superior force of military regulars supported by Native allies, the early years of the French and Indian War all favored the French. (With the exception of the Iroquois, most Northeast tribes sided with the French.) However, the balance of power shifted dramatically when William Pitt was named British Prime Minister in 1756. With the vast Americas offering almost unlimited opportunity for settlement and expansion, as well as extraordinary natural resources, Pitt saw victory in North America as the key element in reaching the English goal of worldwide supremacy. So he began to pour resources into the region.

In 1759 a climactic battle was fought on the Plains of Abraham in Quebec. Led by General James Wolfe, the English finally defeated the French forces under General Montcalm. Sporadic fighting continued for another year until Montreal was captured by General Jeffery Amherst (whose name is still familiar because of the eponymous Massachusetts town). This essentially ended France's colonial exploitation of North America. Having lost their sponsor, Native Americans in the region ceased to be a serious threat to renewed settlement. The hostilities officially ended with the 1763 Treaty of Paris. Britain was now the dominant world power, but at a fearful financial and administrative cost. Twelve

---

15 Robert R. Brooks, "Chapter One, The First Fifty Years," Williamstown, The First Two Hundred Years, 1753–1953 (Williamstown Historical Commission, Second Edition, 1974).

years later the emboldened American colonies would rise up and successfully defeat their fatally weakened master.

FIGHTING THE BRITISH

—

In 1765 the British began to levy sales taxes on imported goods, to help them finance the rising costs of stationing troops and maintaining control over the colonies. In retaliation, the Americans ceased purchasing English goods whenever possible. Matters grew violent in early 1770 when frightened British troops fired into an unruly Boston crowd, killing five. Three years later, in response to an egregious tax on tea, protestors dumped ninety thousand pounds of British tea into Boston Harbor. British Lt. General Thomas Gage headed from New York to Boston with reinforcements to regain control, and on April 18, 1775, an army of seven hundred British regulars marched on Concord, Massachusetts, intending to crush the pending rebellion before it started. They were repulsed at Lexington by volunteer militia, and the long-simmering Revolutionary War was finally under way.

At first, it seemed impossible that a ragtag collection of settlers could successfully engage and ultimately defeat the trained and seasoned British regulars, who were augmented by Hessian German mercenaries. However, in the fall of 1774, in anticipation of the conflict, the colonies had started to train for war. Throughout the Commonwealth of Massachusetts, including East (later Adams) and West (later Williamstown) Hoosac, Committees of Correspondence and Safety were formed to transform farmers into soldiers. Our ancestors were hardened men; many were farmers and expert marksmen, who had learned to live and hunt off the land just for survival. In previous conflicts with the French and Natives, they had learned to employ guerrilla tactics against the regimented British soldiers, and were far better prepared for the type of warfare that was about to begin. Above all, they had the incentive of fighting for their own land.

When word of the fighting to the east reached the western Massachusetts communities, members of the different local militia regiments immediately began marching towards Boston to join the fray, some as individuals and others as part of organized companies. The earliest to reach the front was a regiment raised over the previous year in Lenox and led by Yale-educated Colonel John Patterson, who served with distinction throughout the war. Another Berkshire regiment was commanded by South Williamstown blacksmith Captain Samuel Sloan, with twenty-nine militiamen from Williamstown and another thirty from surrounding towns. Both regiments participated in the bloody Battle of Bunker Hill on June 17, when the British prevailed, but each side sustained huge losses (more than one thousand British and four hundred colonists). They later became part of Patterson's 26th Regiment in the Continental Army. History also cites North Village (later North Adams) resident Josiah Holbrook for single-handedly capturing thirteen Hessian soldiers during the 1777 Battle of Bennington. Meanwhile, Oliver Parker's tavern in the North Village supplied room and board, often without compensation, for soldiers passing through the village on the way to battle General Burgoyne at Fort Ticonderoga.[16]

During the early part of the war, when victory by either side remained very much in doubt, the Continental Army, under

---

16   W. F. Spear, History of North Adams, Massachusetts: 1749-1885 (North Adams, Massachusetts: Hoosac Valley News Printing House, 1885), pp. 20, 21.

Commander-in-Chief General George Washington, gradually increased both in strength and fighting ability. The war ended in the north in early October 1777, when British General John Burgoyne surrendered his entire force of six thousand troops to American Major General Horatio Gates in Saratoga, New York. In February 1778, France, led by the Marquis de Lafayette, joined the war on the side of the patriots. So the colonists' once-deadly enemy was now their ally. Fighting continued in the south, west, and at sea for nearly four more years, but the Americans, aided by the French, finally prevailed at Yorktown, Virginia, where British General Charles Cornwallis surrendered on October 19, 1781. The war officially ended with the signing of the Treaty of Paris on September 3, 1783.

Now free of British rule, the thirteen colonies set about creating a new nation. However, they faced the staggering cost of the war. Estimated American military deaths from all causes numbered more than twenty-five thousand, not including fourteen hundred missing, compared to ten thousand British. Many continental soldiers ended up penniless, having received little or no pay during their service, and the country itself was deeply in debt, a burden which wouldn't be paid off until the early 1800s, primarily through taxation. The strained British economy scarcely fared better and, irony of irony, by 1779 France was basically bankrupt. This, along with deep festering problems related to social injustice, led to the French Revolution.[17]

As the victorious Americans licked their wounds, settlement and industrialization of New England began again in earnest.

---

17   Spear, pp. 20, 21.

SETTLING THE BERKSHIRES

—

While continual warfare was a major contributor to the slow pace of growth in the northwest corner of Massachusetts, so was the geography of the region. The Hoosac Mountains to the east protected it from the rest of the state, while to the west the Taconic Range separated it from New York State. Accordingly, while English settlers founded Springfield, Northampton, Hatfield, and Hadley along the Connecticut River in Massachusetts between 1636 and 1670, Adams wasn't incorporated until over one hundred years later, even though only fifty miles to the north.

In 1733, Sheffield became the first town incorporated in western Massachusetts. A year later, missionary John Sergeant began his ministry in Indian Town, which was incorporated in 1739 as Stockbridge. Over fifteen years he baptized more than half of the some two hundred Mohicans living in the area. Later, the Massachusetts General Court ruled that this land could never be sold, a reward for the tribe's assistance against the French during the French and Indian War, and later against the British during the Revolutionary War. However, the "reward" was short-lived, as settlers moved into the area following the Revolution. The tribe was eventually relocated, first to New York State and later to Wisconsin.[18]

At the request of the Massachusetts General Court, in May 1739 Ephraim Williams Sr. (father of Colonel Williams Jr.) and two associates surveyed the townships of Clarksburg, East Hoosac,

---

18 David J. McLaughlin, The Unfolding History of the Berkshires (Pentacle Press, Second Edition 2007), pp. 14–17, 20–23.

and West Hoosac. Although the map they prepared was apparently never used in laying out the new townships, this was the first foray of the Williams family into the Berkshire wilderness.[19] They soon returned.

A second survey made in 1749 did in fact lay out East Hoosac, measuring seven miles north to south by five miles east to west, the only area town created with such a regular form. Future settlers were also faced with some stringent requirements. The first minister received one sixty-third of the total property, with two sixty-thirds set aside for the ministry and schools. The remaining property was then divided into sixty equal parts for settlement. Each settler had to furnish a bond of twenty British pounds sterling (roughly US $30,000 today), pay an equal portion of the cost of surveying and preparing the tract for settlement, build a proper dwelling before the end of three years, and develop six acres for agriculture within five years. Because of the continuing threat from the French and their Native allies, initially there were few takers, and the houses that were built were made of hewn logs rather than the specified sawed boards.[20]

However, once fear of the Native Americans had largely dissipated, the desire for new settlements reawakened at a frantic pace, and despite the mountainous barriers, many of them were sited in Berkshire County, which was established in 1761. Between then and 1779, some twenty new towns were incorporated, including Pittsfield and Great Barrington (1761), Williamstown and Lanesborough (1765), and Hancock (1776).

---

19   McLaughlin, p. 1.

20   North Adams and Vicinity Illustrated (Special Edition of the North Adams Transcript, 1897), p. 13.

Replica of 1853 House in Williamstown
Photo by author

In June 1762, the township of East Hoosac, along with nine
other townships, was sold at auction for 3,180 British pounds
to Nathan Jones, with Colonel Elisha Jones and John Murray as
partners. In the fall of that year, forty-eight building lots of one
hundred acres each were laid out along the Hoosic River and its
southern branch. In 1776, twenty more lots were laid out, and
Israel Jones was authorized to bring in an initial sixty settlers.
Two years later, the remaining pieces of land were sold. The town
thus created was incorporated as Adams on October 15, 1778,
in honor of Revolutionary War hero Samuel Adams, and the
first town meeting was held in March of the following year. The

inhabitants numbered roughly five hundred, the majority having come from Connecticut and Rhode Island just before the Revolutionary War. Nearly all the initial settlers were located in the South Village (today's Adams) where the land was better suited for farming than to the north. Prior to 1785, there were only five homes in the North Village (which became North Adams), occupied by Giles Barnes, Josiah Wright, Eli Colton, Samuel Day, and William Farrand. They were congregated at the foot of what is now Main Street and the intersection of State Street/Marshall Street, not far from where 87 Marshall Street is located. Ten years later, there were still only a dozen or so buildings, with Jeremiah Colegrove Sr., Israel Jones, David Darling, and David Estes being the major landowners.[21]

The region was heavily forested, and conditions were extraordinarily primitive: barter was the principal method of trade, and purchased commodities had to be hand-carried from Williamstown. As trees were cleared to build the North Village, the removal of tree trunks was at first neglected. Later, working with teams of horses, groups of roughly fifty men were organized to clear the stumps from Main Street. The early North Village was referred to as "Slab City," since the first houses were constructed using slabs left over from the primitive lumbering operations. Growth was hindered by the lack of both capital and adequate transportation. Settlers were very poor and operated nearly self-sufficient farms, also doing their own spinning and weaving. The only "roads" were muddy, rutted thoroughfares, often little more than widened former Native trails filled with rocks and the residue of fallen trees. Initially, most stretched only north and south between today's North Adams and Adams, and west to

---

21   Spear, History of North Adams, pp. 1–5.

Williamstown, until a trail was built over Hoosac Mountain. It was a major milestone when stagecoach service began over the mountains between Greenfield and Albany in 1814. This consisted of "a lumbering uncovered wagon jolting over the stumps and rocks heralded by vigorous blasts on a tin horn".[22] The first train service, between North Adams and Pittsfield, didn't commence until 1846.

If superior farming conditions initially led early settlers to concentrate on the South Village, eventually the superior water power created by the Hoosic River—which was much wider and more powerful than today—led to economic ascendancy in the north. Industry began modestly in the early 1750s, when small saw and grist mills were built along the river branches. Since wheat was a staple in the settlers' diet, and lumber was desperately needed as construction material, the initial output of these primitive mills was used for survival rather than commerce.

Textile manufacturing was the obvious next step, and as settlement and industrialization of New England began in earnest, Adams was ready to develop into an industrial powerhouse in the secluded northwest corner of Massachusetts.

---

22   North Adams and Vicinity Illustrated, p. 14.

CHAPTER TWO

THE INDUSTRIALIZATION OF NORTH ADAMS

Early industrialization of the North Village of Adams started slowly, enabled by surging water power from the north and south branches of the Hoosic River that converged near the center of what is now downtown North Adams. First, dams were built and mills placed adjacent to the resulting falls. The mechanical energy of the rotating water wheel was translated to the turning of the grinding plates in a grist mill, the up-and-down motion of a saw in a lumber mill, or to accomplish a variety of other tasks. In the European textile industry in the late 1700s, much more efficient steam engines slowly began to assume many of these tasks, following the invention of the steam-powered loom by Edmund Cartwright[1]. In the early 1800s, electric power as we know it didn't exist, and practical electric motors weren't available until the 1880s (North Adams native and electrical inventor Frank J. Sprague was a pioneer in the development of constant speed electric motors), nor was the use first of arc and then incandescent lamps for lighting purposes. In the Berkshires, water was still used to power most machinery and candles and whale oil provided light in village houses up to the mid-1800s. This might sound quaintly idyllic, but life was extremely hard.

---

1   Edmund Cartwright, *World Book 2004*.

If water was a welcome early source of power, it was also a curse when spring floods swept through the valleys, wiping out many of the incipient dams and mills along the river banks. These were rebuilt again and again as the settlers gradually learned how to deal with the torrents. Periodic flooding continued all the way into the mid-twentieth century, when the US Army Corps of Engineers finally constructed effective flood control sluiceways along the north and south branches of the Hoosic River. Abundant water also fulfilled another essential function, offering an easy solution to waste disposal. Unfortunately, this led to major problems involving contamination of the waterways, especially as the textile industry became the major economic engine.

Fibers from the flax plant were used to make linen cloth, but in the early Berkshires textile industry the raw materials were primarily cotton (from the south) and wool (from herds of Merino sheep imported from France or Spain and held in pastures around the North Village[2]). First the raw fibers had to be cleaned and densified ("fulling"). Then the disorganized fibers were aligned roughly parallel to each other ("carding") prior to the spinning process, which created the yarn used in the subsequent cloth-weaving process (first done by hand and then by increasingly complex looms). Later, colors and patterns were added to the cloth ("printing"), and it was finally sewn into clothing or other items[3].

From humble beginnings, over time this homespun cottage industry was replaced by factories that manufactured cloth;

---

2 Timothy Christopher Coogan II, *The Forging of a New Mill Town: North and South Adams, MA, 1780–1860* (NYU PhD Thesis, 1992), p. 112.

3 Textiles, *World Book 2004*.

more complex operations were introduced as cloth printing became the dominant textile industry in North Adams. By the late nineteenth century, Arnold Print Works dominated the local economy. Still, these were risky businesses continually threatened by floods, destruction by fire in the easily combustible mills and factories, domestic and offshore competition, periodic recessionary cycles in the United States and overseas, and war.

Initially, because of severely limited transportation, towns such as the North and South Villages of Adams were forced to be self-sufficient, and a host of ancillary businesses were developed to support the growing textile industry: blacksmith shops, carpenter shops, cooperages, and machine shops, to name just a few. Tanneries and shoe manufacturing also became popular local industries. Eventually, the cost of labor and electricity—which by the early twentieth century had become the primary source of power—forced many of these businesses to seek cheaper locations in the south and then eventually out of the country. Following the 1929 depression, Adams and North Adams were almost ghost towns, like so many other New England mill towns. Then electronics arrived in the form of the Sprague Specialties Company (later renamed the Sprague Electric Company), and with the advent of World War II the economy surged. Sprague dominated the local economy for the next fifty years, before labor strife, offshore competition, and questionable strategic decisions combined to cause its demise.

Because of the topography of the area and the fact that the land to both the west and south of the North Village was superior for farming, initially Williamstown and the South Village grew much more rapidly. By the end of the eighteenth century the South Village was one of the most rapidly growing townships in the Berkshires. Because of thin, rocky soil, North-Enders found that lumber was a much easier way to make a living, and lumber mills and grist mills for wheat began to spring up along the edges of the river branches as early as the 1760s. Few survived, and many were destroyed by the raging floods of the 1770s and 1780s. However, what became known as "the age of artisans" began in the North township in the mid-1790s, as skilled craftsmen such as Jeremiah Colegrove, David Estes, Edward Richmond, Giles Tinker, Artemas Crittenden, Caleb Turner, and others began to move into the area, mostly from Connecticut and Rhode Island. Young and ambitious, they brought with them a wealth of practical knowledge and Yankee ingenuity, especially in the textile industry.

BEGINNINGS

—

Although there were earlier mills, Captain Jeremiah Colegrove deserves most of the credit for founding the textile industry in the North Village. He was born in Rhode Island in 1758 and started work as a blacksmith. Tall and athletic, he served in the Revolutionary Army as a gunsmith, although he never saw combat. He moved to the North Village in 1794 and, with his brother-in-law Elisha Brown, purchased property near Fort Massachusetts as well as additional acreage near the center of downtown North Adams. He introduced improved methods of harnessing water power, built a mill to manufacture flaxseed oil and, in 1795, built the first blacksmith shop within the city limits. The later addition of machinery for fulling and dressing led to the primitive manufacture of wool cloth. Then, along with Benjamin Sibley, John Waterman, and several others, in 1810 he founded the first corporation in the North Village, the Adams North Village Cotton and Woolen Manufacturing Company. It was located in a two-story brick building erected along the Hoosic River on the west side of Marshall Street. Much of the process, such as separation of cotton seeds from the fibers and use of hand looms to make cloth, was still done as a cottage industry in local households. The factory handled the fulling process, carding of the fibers, and finally spinning the fibers into thread. Such a "mill" was really a small village with a dam, millrace, the factory and its machinery, housing for some of the factory workers, and usually a store. In this manner, as it grew North Adams became a collection of villages, each with an ethnic diversity built around the origin of its immigrant workers. The company operated until around the 1860s[4].

Besides Colegrove, other textile mills and related businesses were both figuratively and actually testing the waters. In 1801, adapting what he had learned from visits to Rhode Island and textile mills elsewhere, creative artisan David Estes built the first carding and cloth-dressing factory in the county. Much of the machinery was purchased from Giles Tinker who, after moving from Lyme, Connecticut, in 1804, started building rudimentary textile manufacturing equipment in partnership with Captain E. Richmond[5].

Textile manufacturing was rapidly becoming the most important industry in the North Village, but the manufacture of cloth was still carried out by local women in their homes. This changed gradually as the first spinning mills began to appear. The first of these was the Old Brick Factory, located at the intersection of Marshall and Main. It was managed by Josiah Q. Robinson and just prior to the War of 1812 employed forty operators produc-

---

4   *North Adams and Vicinity Illustrated*, p. 16

5   Ibid.

ing cotton cloth using hand looms. The second was William E. Brayton's Eagle Factory, located at the intersection where Eagle Street crossed the north branch of the Hoosic River. Additional mills also began to operate in both the North and South Villages. Still, the use of hand looms provided the only process available for manufacturing cloth, whether carried out in factories or outsourced to local families. Caleb Turner introduced his own design of a water-powered loom in 1818, but it wasn't until the 1823 introduction of the first Satinet (a faux satin-like fabric made from cotton) water-powered looms by Salmon Burlingame (who later went on to found Burlingame and Darby's, the first hardware and drug store in the North Village) that hand-weaving finally began to disappear. In the meantime, foreign politics and continuing warfare took a devastating toll on the infant textile industry[6].

The American Revolution ended in 1783, although the peace was an uneasy one as the British continued to occupy American territory along the Great Lakes, supporting Native American tribes against the settlers in the frontier territory, and imposing unfavorable commercial agreements upon the former colonies. The seemingly endless European warfare that continued between Britain and France from 1792 to 1815 led to major disruption of American shipping, as the British attempted to blockade any shipments to France, and the French, under Napoleon Bonaparte, did the same to the British Isles. Although the United States had prospered by shipping to both sides in the conflict, by 1806 these blockades began to threaten the very financial underpinnings of the young country. Under pressure from a group of some twenty young and aggressive Democratic Republicans (known as the War Hawks), who were mostly from the south and west, it

---

6 Coogan, *The Forging of a New Mill Town*, pp. 171–176.

seemed that once more armed conflict was the only solution, as on June 18, 1812, President James Madison declared war on the United Kingdom.

The United States was ill-prepared both militarily and economically for the War of 1812. Despite some successes on the high seas by American frigates such as the USS Constitution and USS United States, by 1814 the American cause had become desperate and appeared lost. Then Captain Thomas MacDonough destroyed a powerful force of ten thousand veteran British troops who were heading south to occupy New York City in a naval battle on Lake Champlain.

Sick of unsuccessfully fighting their former colonists, the British had had enough. On December 24, 1814, the two countries signed the Treaty of Ghent (it was ratified on February 17, 1815), officially ending the War of 1812. However, word didn't reach New Orleans in time to prevent the Americans' greatest victory, as an eclectic force under Major General "Old Hickory" Jackson—the future US president—destroyed a massive British force attacking the city[6].

After the Treaty of Ghent the British and Americans never again attempted to settle their grievances militarily, but an even more insidious economic warfare began as the British started dumping cloth and textile goods into the US at prices well below those of local industries. During the post-war recession from 1819 to 1821, most of the textile factories throughout the Northeast, including those in the Berkshires, were forced to close.

By the mid-1820s there were some nineteen textile factories in the North and South Villages of Adams employing more than five hundred workers. However, the opening of the Erie Canal in

1825 only made things worse, as low-cost goods from the west began to inundate the area, and only the very fittest were able to survive; it would take decades before the northern Berkshires textile industry again became truly viable. Yet some clever artisans, such as Giles Tinker, were able to weather the storm by supplying hand- carding and weaving machinery to area families for use in making cloth for local consumption[7].

While cotton was the main pillar of the textile industry, it was followed by wool. The first woolen mill was established by Artemas Crittenden in 1813, and the second by Sanford Blackinton, Rufus Wells, and Joseph White after they left the employ of Crittenden in the early 1820s. They located in what is today the Blackinton neighborhood of North Adams, and by the end of the century the Blackinton Company was successfully manufacturing a line of worsteds and fine cashmeres. The North Adams Manufacturing Company was started in 1831 by William E. and Dr. Thomas C. Brayton. They purchased land on the river just west of North Adams, in what became the hamlet of Braytonville, and built a three-story stone mill fitted out with equipment from Giles Tinker. After several reorganizations and management changes, by the end of the nineteenth century the company was manufacturing fine cashmeres, cheviots, and worsteds, and the population of Braytonville had reached one thousand[8]. Today, the building is the home of the Excelsior Printing Company.

There were other woolen mills in the North Village, but, like the cotton mills, few survived the fierce pressure of the marketplace. Both cotton and woolens continued their sporadic existence until

---

7   Coogan, p. 208.

8   *North Adams and Vicinity Illustrated*, p. 17.

cloth-printing began to dominate the North Adams economy. In 1829, Caleb B. Turner and Walter Laflin manufactured by hand the first piece of printed cloth in the Berkshires. Over the next seventy years and through numerous ownership, management, and name changes, the firm evolved to become the Windsor Print Works with its main facility located towards the western end of Union Street. By the end of the 1800s, it employed close to eight hundred people. Other businesses followed, including the Johnson Manufacturing Co., formed by Sylvander Johnson, Nathaniel Hathaway, George Bly, and Peter Blackinton, which employed three hundred fifty by the end of the century. They all started as calico print works, but none survived to dominate the cloth-printing industry as did the subject of the next chapter, Arnold Print Works.

As the textile industry matured, labor strife began to play a significant part in the industrial history of North Adams. A 1992 New York University PhD thesis by Timothy C. Coogan II[9] provides an interesting perspective on the subject, as well as insight into what work in the textile mills was really like. It is not a pretty picture. Purely because of geography, the early textile industry in the northern Berkshires developed more slowly and remained largely a cottage industry for a longer period of time than in the impersonal factory cities in Rhode Island, Connecticut, and, for example, Lowell, Massachusetts, and Nashua, New Hampshire. Still, by the mid-1850s the efficiency of the factory system began to dominate even in the North and South Villages of Adams, as employment moved from local residents to imported labor, first from surrounding villages in the Berkshires and southern Vermont, and then from elsewhere.

---

9   Coogan, *The Forging of a New Mill Town*.

Seeking what she believed to be a better life, a girl could start working in the mills at twelve years of age or even younger[10]. She earned around fifty cents per week (plus room and board) and worked every day except Sunday from six o'clock in the morning to half past eight at night. By the age of sixteen, she could earn $1.50 a week or a little more. Initially she probably lodged in a private household, rather than the tenements and boardinghouses found in the larger textile cities, though by the mid-1850s the number of employees forced even this local advantage to disappear. Yet, for the ethnic immigrant groups that began to populate the factories, working conditions and pay were still better than where they came from. The mill owners found that the French Canadians, who first populated the Beaver area of North Adams, were particularly ideal employees since they expected the entire family, including young children, to toil in the factories[11].

Even if working conditions in New England textile factories were an improvement over sweatshops in Italy, Ireland, and Quebec, the seeds of labor unrest had already been planted well before the immigrants began to arrive. Following an 1838 visit to the North Village, novelist Nathaniel Hawthorne sensed that the labor peace was about to unravel, and described his impressions in *The American Notebooks* in 1868[12]. He wrote that the large factories,

---

10 The child labor abuse that existed in New England factories and elsewhere in the US into the early twentieth century has been well documented. See, for example, the Lewis Hine Project at morningsonmaplestreet.com. In August 2011 there was an excellent related exhibition at the Brill Gallery in North Adams.

11 Janet E. Roberts, *A History of the French Canadians in North Adams* (Williams College History Honors Thesis, April 1975), p. 12.

12 Nathaniel Hawthorne, The American Notebooks (Boston: Ticknor and Fields, 1868).

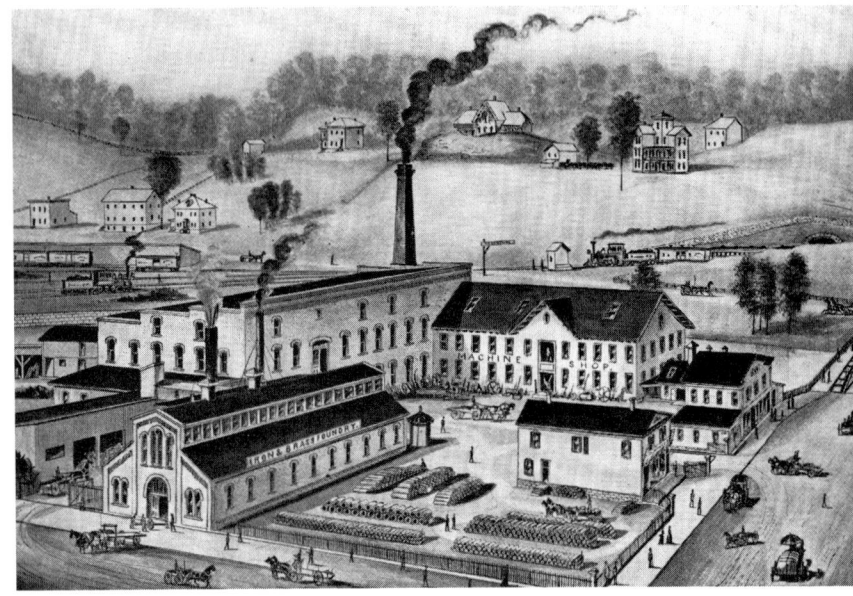

James Hunter Machine Company, circa 1870
Image courtesy of the Hunter Family

some having "two, three, or more (large) boarding houses near them," seemed utterly out of place "in the midst of such wild scenery." By the time of the Civil War, Coogan observes, "Adams emerged as one of the nation's most radical communities, particularly (in) its frequencies of strikes."[13]

It was inevitable that, as the factories grew larger, the initial paternalism would begin to break down, and the long hours, low pay, and difficult and dangerous working conditions—as well as the impersonal living conditions—would finally take their toll. Per-

---

13   Coogan, The Forging of a New Mill Town, p. 42.

haps an additional contributing factor was a change in the make-up of the population; although initially relatively homogenous, by 1855 more than 20 percent of the seven thousand inhabitants of Adams (North and South) were foreign born[14]. Following the textile industry recession caused by the repeal of protective tariffs in the mid-1840s, the first social breakdown in the North Village took place in 1853, when Oliver Arnold & Company's mill operators staged a two-day strike. As discussed in the next chapter, after the worldwide depression that began in the United States in 1857, things became much worse, and eventually industrial action would play a vital role in the history of 87 Marshall Street, Arnold Print Works, and Sprague Electric.

JAMES HUNTER MACHINE COMPANY

—

In the early 1830s, along the twin branches of the Hoosic River, fifty or more mills manufactured cotton and woolen goods, lumber, grist, calico cloth, and flaxseed oil, all competing for space with tanneries, furnaces, forges, and equipment manufacturers. While Giles Tinker was the first to offer competitive textile manufacturing equipment, it was the James Hunter Machine Company that eventually dominated this industry locally, successfully remaining in business for nearly 135 years.

Founder James Hunter began his textile apprenticeship at the age of fifteen in 1821 in Galashiels, Scotland (by pure coincidence nearly 150 years later, Sprague Electric opened an aluminum capacitor plant in Galashiels). In 1833, Hunter left Scotland with his family for the New World, landing in Quebec and after sev-

---

14   Coogan, p. 428.

JAMES HUNTER
1806 - 1891

Founder of the James Hunter
Machine Company, 1847, and
its first President.

JAMES E. HUNTER
1830 - 1919

Son of the Founder of the Company, second President. He
invented among many other
things, one of the first Variable
Speed Mechanisms in this
country.

James Hunter Machine Company, first presidents
Image courtesy of the Hunter Family

eral moves ending up in North Adams as a superintendent in the Brown & Tyler Print Works. A failed partnership in a cotton mill followed, and then in 1847 he started to make machinery castings in an old furnace property on Main Street. There followed a series of different company names, partnerships, and product offerings, including establishment of a small machine shop in 1851. In 1857, he formed a partnership with his son, twenty-seven-year-old James E. Hunter (who had been working with his father in different capacities since he was eight years old), and M. C. Jewett to form an equipment manufacturing firm. James E. became president after his father's death in 1891, and successive generations of company presidents were all family members, also named James Hunter but with different middle names. In 1891, the firm was incorporated as the James Hunter Machine Company, the name it maintained until its closure in 1983.

One of the earliest and most important product lines was power transmission equipment, which was initially sold to local mills. Using ropes, belts, pulleys, couplings, and similar paraphernalia, such equipment was used to transfer the energy from a rotating water wheel shaft to the different pieces of textile equipment and later to generate electricity. Soon the company began to add an increasingly broad line of textile machinery, which fueled its growth. As the company grew, the headquarters location was an ever-expanding complex of buildings in the prime downtown location at the corner of Main Street and State Street, only a few blocks south of 87 Marshall Street. The family continued to lead the firm, and by 1957 James H. ("Bing") Hunter, a good friend of Sprague Electric's Robert C. Sprague, was president.

A handsome one-hundredth anniversary album published in 1947, *Heritage of Dependability*, traces the history of the company, listing a broad inventory of some fifty different types of equipment and products, sold to customers in more than twenty countries around the world. Like the Sprague Electric Company, Hunter Machine also emphasized quality and was uncompromising in meriting its logo, *Built by Hunter—It's Dependable*[15].

Yet by the late 1950s the company was facing increased pressure from the federal government to improve the environmental quality of its now-aging foundry operations, and in 1960 the James Hunter Machine Company was sold to Crompton & Knowles Corporation, which seven years later moved its main facility to a handsome new location on South Church Street. In 1971, the original site on Main Street was donated to the City of North Adams, and the property is now the location of the North Adams City Hall.

In 1972, as Crompton & Knowles's diversification strategy gathered steam and it planned to close or sell all of the acquired Hunter Machine locations, the Hunter family bought back the company, but new problems created further havoc. By the end of the 1970s, a strengthening US dollar was damaging export sales, and product liability insurance premiums were becoming prohibitive. With no other solution apparent, in 1983 the company closed its doors for good, leaving behind a legacy as one of the finest companies of its kind in the world[16]. In many ways, the demise of Hunter Machine bears an eerie similarity to what happened to Sprague Electric at roughly the same time. Today, the Hunter family contributes handsomely to local philanthropy, with its contributions to the success of MASS MoCA recognized in the naming of one of the museum's main spaces, the Hunter

---

15 *Heritage of Dependability*, James Hunter Machine Co. 100th Anniversary Album, 1947.

16 "Jimmie" Hunter provided an interesting perspective on the relationship between Hunter Machine and Crompton & Knowles.

Center for Performing Arts.

FOOTWEAR FACTORIES

—

Although employment numbers never rivaled those of the textile and equipment industries, shoe manufacturing was another principal local trade that lasted in North Adams until the 1970s. The first shoe factory was formed by Edwin Childs and David C. Rogers in 1843. Following a series of relocations, expansions, and management changes, the company became known as Whitman & Millard, and by the end of the nineteenth century Henry S. Millard was the sole proprietor, operating in a brick factory on Union Street built at the end of the Civil War. The principal line was women's shoes[17]. In 1920, the Wall-Streeter Shoe Company—founded in 1912 by James Wall, Ed Streeter, and Albert Doyle—bought the Millard building and continued operations for another fifty years, employing an average of two hundred people. In 1974, Wall-Streeter was purchased by Florsheim Shoe Co., which shortly thereafter closed the North Adams facility. Then-president Robert E. Wall, who died in 1992, was a very good friend of the Sprague family. As described in a later chapter, during World War II the Wall-Streeter Shoe Company and Sprague Specialties Company cooperated to manufacture gas masks in one of Sprague's North Adams plants.

Just before the end of the nineteenth century, another half-dozen shoe manufacturers were operating in North Adams. The most prominent of these was the C. T. Sampson Shoe Company, which at the time specialized in medium- and fine-grade shoes for

---

17   *North Adams and Vicinity Illustrated*, p. 17.

men, women, and children; with between five and six hundred employees, it had the capacity to produce five thousand pairs of shoes a day. The main facility was on Marshall Street, right across from number 87, where the Northern Berkshire District Court and North Adams Office of Social Security Administration now occupy the former Sprague Electric R&D Center.

Like almost all of his contemporaries, Calvin T. Sampson learned his trade from the bottom up when, as a young man, he started selling shoes from door to door. In 1851, he opened a retail store at the corner of Eagle and Main; following a fire that destroyed the building, in 1853 he rebuilt on the property and started to manufacture shoes, concentrating initially on women's footwear. As the business grew, in the late 1860s he moved to a large multi-storied building on Marshall Street. Originally built to house a cutlery company, the building stood empty, and Sampson was able to buy it for a song.

One of the firm's most interesting legacies stems from labor problems with a trade organization known as the Crispins in late 1869 and early 1870. The union was planning a strike for higher wages, although Sampson already thought that his employees' pay was exorbitant. In retaliation, he hired replacement Chinese workers from San Francisco, the first seventy-five of whom arrived in June 1870, and a year later numbered around one hundred twenty-five. The expected retaliatory labor strife never developed, and the Chinese proved to be excellent workmen. They were all gone by September 1880, when machinery had largely replaced hand labor, and the Crispins were no longer a factor[18]. (In an ironic twist of fate, this period in North Adams's history was memorial-

---

18   *Calvin T. Sampson* (North Adams Historical Society, undated).

ized in a major 2009 MASS MoCA exhibition by Simon Starling, *The Nanjing Particles*. It included a huge 1875 photograph of Chinese workers standing in front of the Sampson building and two large stainless steel forms alleged to represent a million times magnification of two silver particles extracted from the original photograph. To realize the mirror-finished sculpture, the artist dispatched museum director Joseph Thompson to China to have the sculpture manufactured with low-cost labor, in a conceptual play on the labor dynamics of the previous one hundred years.)

OTHER INDUSTRIES

—

As previously mentioned, in 1839 Salmon Burlingame started a hardware and drug business on Main Street. He died in 1883, but by the end of the century Burlingame & Darby's was one of North Adams's most successful businesses, offering an extensive hardware line as well as patent medicines and other drugstore-related items[19].

Light from sources other than hazardous gas lamps became available after the North Adams Gas Light Co. was incorporated in 1864, initially providing gas lighting services to manufacturing entities. Then in 1890, the company added electricity services, following the acquisition of the North Adams Electric Light and Power Company. Two daily and three weekly newspapers kept the population up-to-date, while a cadre of additional professional skills further served the community, including three architects, eight civil engineers/draftsmen, fifteen clergymen, eighteen law firms, four veterinarians, eight dentists, twenty-eight physicians, and, topping the list, eighteen "professional musicians."

---

19   *North Adams and Vicinity Illustrated*, pp. 82–87.

Simon Starling, *Nanjing Particles*, MASS MoCA Gallery 5 installation view
Photo: Elizabeth Berg

By the end of the nineteenth century, North Adams, which had formally split from Adams in 1878, was a vibrant, growing city with a population of between twenty and twenty-five thousand (in contrast, today there are fewer than fourteen thousand inhabitants). *North Adams & Vicinity Illustrated, 1897* provides a staggering amount of detail and statistics on just how diversified the city had become. Besides those already discussed, there was a wide variety of additional businesses, including tanneries and manufacturers of such diverse items as boxes, washing machines, clothing, building materials, cabinetry, and carriages, to name just a few. There were eight hotels, including the one-hundred-room Wilson House on Main Street, ten restaurants and, sounding more like a Wild West town than a New England City, nineteen saloons. The Hoosac Valley Street Railway Co. provided electric trolley service connecting Adams, North Adams, Williamstown, and eventually Bennington, Vermont; following the 1876 completion of the Hoosac Tunnel, no less than six separate railway systems connected the town to the outside world.

However, the names of several additional important enterprises still resonate on the Main Street of North Adams. Clarksburg-born H. W. Clark entered the wholesale grocery business in 1873 on Holden Street and, after outgrowing the business, built the Flatiron Building at the corner of State and Summer streets, where three generations of Clarks successfully operated the H. W. Clark Wholesale Company. An 1899 expansion into the bakery business led to two additional factories for the manufacture of crackers and biscuits. Following a 1913 fire, all operations were consolidated on Ashland Street. While keeping the Clark name, the firm was sold in 1928 and ten years later merged with the Atlantic Biscuit Co. and Maine Biscuit Co., creating one of the largest independent biscuit companies in the US. Like so many other former New England factories, the Ashland Street facility has become an apartment complex.

In 1870, twenty-year-old Charles H. Cutting started to operate what became North Adams's best-known clothing store. Initially primarily a men's shop, associated stores were opened in Orange, Adams, and Athol, and in 1896 a large children's clothing line was added in North Adams. C. H. Cutting & Co. operated in North Adams until 1960, when it was replaced by another clothing store, W. G. Roberts Co. Today, the space is home to several very different entities, including the Massachusetts Registry of Motor Vehicles.

Yet throughout most of the nineteenth century, the name most associated with North Adams was that of its premier manufacturer, Arnold Print Works.

CHAPTER THREE

ARNOLD PRINT WORKS

Despite being only a few years old, the Sprague Specialties Company was already well-established when it moved to North Adams in 1929. Arnold Print Works, on the other hand, was a purely North Adams creation. Three Arnold brothers—Oliver, Harvey, and John F.—founded the enterprise, but were forced into bankruptcy following the Civil War. With financial support from David A. Brayton, Albert C. Houghton stepped in, first as treasurer, and by the end of the 1870s as the major stockholder and managing director.

Over the next twenty-five years, the rise of Arnold Print Works was nothing short of meteoric, and by the beginning of the twentieth century the company was the largest and most successful textile printing enterprise in the world. Yet only six years later, a disastrous cotton speculating scheme initiated by Houghton just before the 1907 recession nearly destroyed everything he had worked to build.

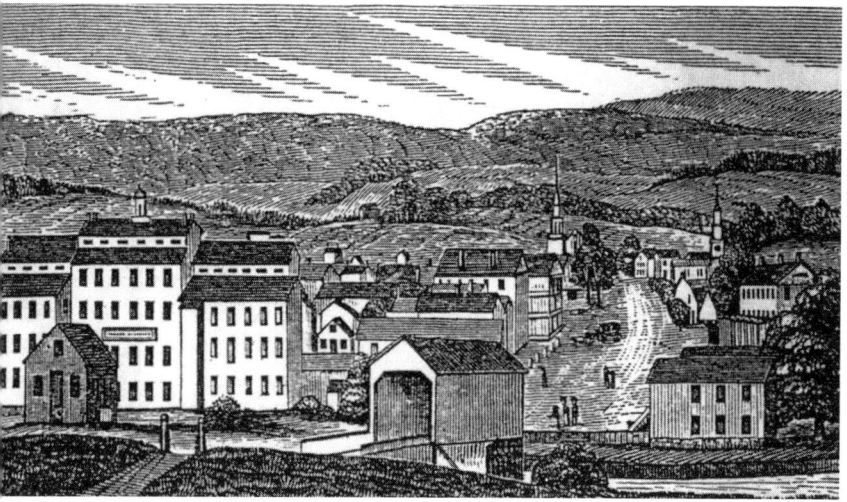

1841 Woodcut of North Adams main street looking east
Image courtesy of North Adams Historical Society

A smaller, different company with new ownership and leadership was able to survive another thirty-five years, and at times even to grow. Then, in 1942, lack of materials and orders during World War II forced the massive North Adams complex at 87 Marshall Street to close its textile printing operations for good. As it turned out, this was just in time for the premises to be absorbed and reopened by the Sprague Specialties/Sprague Electric Company.

When attempting to decipher the beginnings, maturation, and ultimate demise of the textile trade in the northern Berkshires, one is struck by how volatile and tumultuous the industry was. There was a continuous stream of fluctuating and often informal partnerships, ownerships, and relationships. Interests were acquired and divested so often that it must have seemed impossible to know just who was where, doing what. Property was bought and sold, expanded, renovated, sometimes razed or destroyed by fire, and then bought and sold again. Streams of immigrants arrived who, although they came from different ethnic backgrounds and cultures, had to be assimilated: English, Irish, French Canadian, Italian, and many more.

With primitive and dangerous lighting conditions and no such thing as an overhead sprinkler system, buildings and businesses regularly burned to the ground. Financial "panics" rocked the marketplace, and periodic drastic floods swept away everything in their path until the Hoosic River was finally tamed in the 1950s. Only a very few of the fittest, best-managed, and sometimes luckiest enterprises survived the chaos within which they had to operate, but even these eventually succumbed.

THE ARNOLDS
—

The story begins in 1802 when a well-to-do and adventuresome farmer named John Arnold, who would become the grandfather of the founders of the Arnold Print Works, moved to North Adams from Rhode Island with his three sons, Harris, Daniel, and John Jr. One can only speculate on the reasons for the move. Land was certainly cheaper in the just-developing northern Berkshires, or perhaps, like those who headed west in covered wagons to the untamed wilds of Native country, the family simply wanted the chance to start a new life in a new place. At least in the Northeast, Native Americans were no longer perceived as a threat.

John purchased four hundred acres of land and divided it equally between his sons. There is little known of how and where Daniel and John Jr. settled, but Harris first lived in Adams and then moved to North Adams in 1830. It was three of Harris's four sons—the aforementioned Oliver, Harvey, and John F.—who became key figures in laying the foundation of Arnold Print Works. The fourth son, Andrew, was an invalid, and ran a store to support his brothers' textile interests[1].

The oldest brother, Oliver, was born in Natick in 1801, and was just a baby when his family moved to the wilds of the northern Berkshires. His textile apprenticeship began in the 1820s, working for Alvin Sanford, who manufactured textile machinery for Giles Tinker. A partnership with Sanford and Dr. Isaac Hodges (a respected local physician who served only as an investor) to manufacture cotton goods followed, in a leased portion of the Union Woolen Mill. Then, together with his brother, Harvey, and Nathaniel Blinn, Oliver formed Arnold, Blinn & Co. A two-story factory built further up the north branch of the Hoosic River was occupied in 1832, and with later additions became part of what is known as the Eclipse Mill. Three years later, Blinn sold his interest, and the firm was renamed O. and H. Arnold.

Harvey Arnold was born in 1806, after his father moved to Adams. He attended Wesleyan Academy and then, wanting to pursue a profession in medicine, began studies under Dr. Hodges. Soon afterwards, he married Hodges's daughter. Poor health forced him to abandon his medical career, and he joined Oliver in Arnold, Blinn & Co. From then until Harvey's death in 1876, the brothers remained close business partners in a series of textile ventures that, after the Civil War, led to the creation of Arnold Print Works.

As Oliver's and Harvey's cotton cloth business continued to

---

1   Coogan, The Forging of a New Mill Town, pp. 258–268.

expand, in 1836 they added the Slater Mill to their Eclipse Mill property, but disaster struck when their sole customer, Turner & Laflin, failed during the Panic of 1837[2], forcing the Arnolds into bankruptcy. While Oliver's skills were in technology and Harvey was an administrator, younger brother John F. was an accomplished accountant with excellent financial skills and contacts. He stepped in and soon had his brothers' company running again, now under the name of John F. Arnold. In 1843, the three formed a new partnership named O. Arnold & Co.

Their cloth-printing experience began the following year, in partnership with Jerome B. Jackson and Johnson D. Stewart, in the Union Print Works. In 1856, A. W. Richardson & Co. bought the Union Print Works property and entered into a five-year contract with the Arnolds to supply cotton cloth for the printing operations. Sensing a unique opportunity in the textile printing trade, the brothers purchased property at the intersection of the north and south branches of the Hoosic River—today's 87 Marshall Street. They erected a four-story building in the northern section to serve as their print works when the contract with Richardson & Co. expired in 1861. Now known as Harvey Arnold & Co., this marked the real beginning of the Arnold Print Works. The first printed cotton cloth from the new works came off the line in early 1863, producing calico cloth using the simple and profitable madder or Garancine processes[3].

By this time the nation was in the middle of the most catastrophic war in its history. The first Confederate state seceded from the

2   As used in the 1800s and early 1900s, "Panic" was synonymous with a deep recession or depression.

3   Spear, *History of North Adams*, p. 94.

Union in January 1861, two months after Abraham Lincoln was elected president, and the Civil War began on April 12 when Southern forces attacked and then captured Fort Sumter off the South Carolina coast. The bloody war dragged on for four years until General Robert E. Lee finally surrendered to General Ulysses S. Grant at Appomattox on April 9, 1865. Less than a week later, Lincoln was assassinated. The combined casualties were greater than any other war in American history. In the South approximately 260,000 died, while another 190,000 were wounded; the equivalent numbers for the North were 364,500 and 282,000 respectively.

North Adams did its part. While the town provided soldiers, the North Adams Iron Company supplied pig iron used in the metal plating of the Union ironclad, USS Monitor. The Civil War Soldiers Monument rises in the center of Monument Square at the eastern end of Main Street. This statue of a lone soldier was originally dedicated by the Ladies Aid Society on July 4, 1878, the same year that North Adams separated from Adams. It was rebuilt and rededicated in 1981 and again in 2000. An online honor roll lists some seventy-four names of residents who were killed in action or died from other causes during the conflict.

The needs of the Union Army for boots and uniforms served as a stimulus to both the shoe and textile industries in the North-east, and the related North Adams factories prospered during the Civil War. Arnold was no exception. Because of limited supplies, the price of cotton cloth skyrocketed, more than compensating for increases in the cost of the hard-to-obtain raw cotton. As a result, the Arnold brothers became very wealthy. In 1865, Harvey Arnold joined a group headed by Williams College President Paul Chadbourne to incorporate the Williamstown Manufacturing Company and erect a large brick mill on Cole Avenue, Williamstown, at the intersection with the Hoosic River. As with other such ventures, the Williamstown mill soon developed into a small, self-contained community, complete with tenements and other housing for the workers and management, a store, and a nearby Catholic church. Harvey Arnold was president and principal stockholder, and a year later the Williamstown Manufacturing Company was shipping its entire output of cotton cloth four miles east to Harvey Arnold & Co. on Marshall Street in North Adams, later becoming a wholly owned subsidiary of that company[4]. As the Print Works continued to grow, ownership of captive satellite cotton cloth suppliers was one of the keys to the firm's success. Unfortunately, this would also create major problems for these mills when their sole customer ran into trouble.

By the end of the Civil War, Harvey Arnold & Co. was the largest manufacturing company in North Adams. Despite still being small compared to the massive textile operations to the east in Lowell and Lawrence, Massachusetts, as well as in Rhode Island, by the end of the war Arnold employed close to one hundred workers, and its facility consisted of four buildings and several drying sheds. Product was shipped by freight on a railroad spur that ran from North Adams to Pittsfield. There it was loaded on the Boston, Worcester, and Western Railroad, the east-west main line that ran from Boston through Pittsfield to Albany and points west. In 1859, as part of the overall Hoosac Tunnel project, a new rail line was completed between North Adams and Troy, New York. However, North Adams still awaited completion of the tunnel, which would open up new markets for local industries by connecting the city directly to Boston[5].

---

4   Brooks, Williamstown, p. 106.

5   Carin L. Cole, *Between Two Worlds: The Business Career of Albert C. Houghton* (Williams College American Studies Honors Thesis, May 6, 1991), pp. 20, 21.

Albert C. Houghton
Image courtesy of North Adams Historical Society

ALBERT C. HOUGHTON

—

There was nothing in the genealogy and background of Albert Charles Houghton to indicate what a brilliant businessman he would become. His father, James Houghton, was born in New York State in 1805, one of eleven children, and moved in 1830 to Stamford, Vermont, where he purchased a farm and a store. He had problems with alcohol and over the years was involved in farming, land speculation, and several diverse businesses, none of which were very successful. He died in 1881[6].

Albert was born on April 13, 1844, and grew up on the farm. After attending local schools in nearby Stamford, Vermont, a brief sojourn at Bernardston Academy near Greenfield, Massachusetts, was cut short by family financial problems, and he went to work in his Uncle Charles's general store. He proved an apt pupil and while still a teenager became proprietor; but it was success in land speculation and an early indirect entry into the textile printing industry that set his future course[7].

 In 1865, while only twenty-one years of age, Albert and his brother Royal purchased a mill in Adams and formed the Houghton Acid Works to manufacture the "red liquor" that was a key ingredient in the madder calico printing process. That same year he married Cordelia Smith from back home in Stamford. In 1868, he purchased timberland in nearby Heartwellville, Vermont, and used proceeds from the sale of spruce timber from this property to make his first land purchase in North Adams.

While Houghton continued his profitable land speculation, in 1871 he jumped into the North Adams textile industry, purchasing the Beaver Street mill from S. W. Brayton with partners William W. Gallup, Arthur A. Smith, and Chester A. Bailey. (Nearly sixty years later this mill became the first North Adams headquarters of the Sprague Specialties Company when it moved there from Quincy.) At the time, it supplied cotton cloth solely to Harvey Arnold & Co.

---

6   Cole, *Between Two Worlds*, p. 10.

7   Cole, pp. 1, 25.

Houghton also went into partnership with Harvey Arnold to create the North Pownal Manufacturing Co., another satellite cotton
cloth feeder plant for Harvey's print works. Both of Houghton's
investments had the same sole customer, yet he seemed obliv-
ous to the risks he was assuming and to his limited experience
in textile manufacturing. Unfazed, he uprooted his family from
Stamford to a leased home on Eagle Street in North Adams[8].

Then disaster struck. On December 27, 1872, a fire started in
one of the print works storehouses, apparently caused by spon-
taneous combustion, and destroyed much of the Marshall Street
complex. Not including those in the satellite feeder plants in
Williamstown and North Pownal, and on Beaver Street in North
Adams, 175 employees were immediately without work. The
timing couldn't have been worse, as three years later the nation
drifted into a deep recession. John F. Arnold owned a quarter interest in Harvey Arnold & Co., while Harvey owned the rest, but
lacking both adequate insurance and sufficient personal financial
resources—and perhaps the will—the Arnold brothers were not
up to the task of rebuilding the business. Desperately in need of
capital, in late July 1873 John F. sold his interest to Edward H.
Arnold, another member of the extended Arnold family; earlier,
Harvey and several other prominent North Adams businessmen
had purchased the Richardson paper mill to try and maintain
some sort of income.

Houghton's successful land speculation ventures had made him
wealthy, and he used much of this wealth to invest in the North
Adams textile industry. Suddenly these investments were very
much at risk. However, Houghton also sensed a real opportu-

---

8   Cole, pp. 29, 30.

Hoosac Tunnel West Portal, 1876
Image courtesy of North Adams Historical Society

nity. Ever the optimist, he succeeded in convincing the Arnold
brothers that the facility could and should be rebuilt, and in
August 1873 reconstruction began, with most of the funds
contributed from Houghton's dwindling financial resources. The
first product from the new facility was shipped in January 1874.
Houghton was now manager, and Joseph Bentley, an experienced
printer newly brought in from Rhode Island, was superintendent.
Since the Arnolds still had an excellent reputation and Harvey
remained the principal stockholder, the E. H. Arnold Company
name was maintained, although none of the family had any real
managerial responsibilities. By the end of the year Houghton was
very much in the driver's seat, owning one third of the Beaver

Mill, one third of the North Pownal Manufacturing Co., and one quarter of the Marshall Street works, which he had purchased from Harvey (one-third of Harvey's remaining interest)[9] in a move that ultimately saved the company[10].

Nevertheless, the recession that began in 1873 was still in full swing and the plight of the textile industry throughout New England remained fragile.

THE HOOSAC TUNNEL

—

The idea of a direct transportation route across northern Massachusetts from Boston to the Hudson River was first envisioned in 1819 as a canal system, following the combined courses of the Green and Hoosic River branches through and around the Hoosac Range. This route was soon abandoned as impractical, and in 1851 the Troy and Greenfield Railroad Company began construction of a tunnel directly through the nearly five miles of solid mountain rock. There was great excitement in North Adams, whose inhabitants saw the tunnel as immediately expanding market access to the east for major industries such as textiles and footwear. Not unlike Boston's recent "Big Dig,"[11] the project took much longer (twenty-four years), cost much more (greater than $21 million or between $400 and $500 million in today's dollars), and proved far more dangerous than even the most conser-

---

9   Cole, pp. 34–38.

10   Cole, pp. 34, 35.

11   The name given to the Boston construction project that installed the main elevated north-south thoroughfare underground, and which took much longer than anticipated and ran many billions of dollars over budget.

vative of forecasts. Although there are widely differing estimates of the number of workers killed during construction, 195 is the generally accepted number. Nearly all accidents were violent, most often resulting from cave-ins, fires, and explosions—first from the black powder used for blasting in the early stages and later from George Mowbray's lethal nitroglycerine. The boring of the tunnel was finally completed on November 19, 1874, and the first train passed through the tube on February 9, 1875. Regular service between Boston and Troy began in 1876[12].

Conventional wisdom would indicate that this must have proved a boon to North Adams, and analysis shows that this was indeed true of the spur that opened in mid-1859 between North Adams and Troy. However, at least initially, the eastward tunnel actually hurt North Adams's industries, as major competitors in the northern tier of Massachusetts's industrial cities, such as Fitchburg and Greenfield, were now able to flood North Adams's western markets with lower-priced products. A detailed analysis by Anthony Parise shows that, as a result of the tunnel's opening, growth in both the North Adams textile and footwear industries between 1875 and 1885 was dramatically below the state average. In the next decade, the North Adams footwear industry declined sharply, but textiles surged again (while still slightly below the state average)[13]. Arnold Print Works was a major cause of this recovery.

Although the complex on Marshall Street had been rebuilt with new equipment, processes, and management, the national reces-

---

12   Cole, pp. 40

13   Anthony F. Parise, *North Adams and the Hoosac Tunnel*
     (Williams College Honors Thesis in American Civilization, May 1973), p. 87.

sion raged on, forcing all North Adams industries to make drastic reductions in costs, employment, and wages. It was too little, too late. By mid-1876 most of the local manufacturing concerns, including the Arnolds', had been forced into bankruptcy and, with no customer, the feeder plants had to shut down as well. As a result, each of the original Arnold brothers filed for personal bankruptcy.

Despite the single-customer problem, Houghton concluded that for long-term success he needed to follow the vertical integration model pursued so successfully in the steel industry by Andrew Carnegie and in oil refining by John D. Rockefeller. This would provide complete control over sources of supply, specifications, technology, and economies of scale, affording the ability to offer unique products at competitive prices. As one of the largest creditors and the managing director of the Print Works, Houghton straddled both sides; he had to get the business running again and raise sufficient capital to do so. It became clear at a June 1, 1876, creditors' meeting, during which a tough repayment plan was laid out for the Print Works, its captive feeder plants, and the E. H. Arnold Company, that unless the Marshall Street plant was quickly operational again, at whatever the cost, all bets were off[14].

BRAYTON TO THE RESCUE

—

With Harvey ill and both John and Oliver having sold their interests, the Arnolds were pretty much out of the picture, and Houghton needed to look elsewhere for capital. So he turned to David A. Brayton of the highly successful Durfee Mills in Fall River, Massachusetts. At the time, Durfee was the largest cotton

---

14   Cole, *Between Two Worlds*, pp. 43–51.

printing mill in the United States and also the largest creditor of the Print Works.

A cousin of North Adams's S. W. Brayton, David A. Brayton was twenty years Houghton's senior and had led an eclectic life that included the trading of molasses and sugar in the West Indies, a brief run at the California gold rush, and broad business experience in a variety of areas, including textiles. Because of the success of the Durfee Mills, which he managed with his brother, John, David had accumulated considerable wealth. By nature a skilled risk-taker, and also wanting to protect his interests, Brayton apparently saw a kindred spirit in Albert Houghton and decided to back him.

With a $150,000 investment from Brayton and satisfied creditors, the newly named Arnold Print Works was incorporated in August 1876, with David Brayton as the largest stockholder and president and Albert Houghton as treasurer. Other major stockholders included the New York City sales director, C. G. Evans, William A. Gallup (the son of William Gallup, co-owner of the Beaver Mill), and David A. Brayton Jr. Before long, the younger generation would be in charge[15].

With the printing equipment at Arnold Print Works on Marshall Street once more up and running, the cotton cloth feeder plants were again open for business. By the end of 1877, profits from the parent company and Beaver Mill allowed Houghton to continue his vertical integration strategy, re-taking control of Williamstown Manufacturing Company, North Pownal Manufacturing Company, and Beaver Mill, and to continue expan-

---

15   Cole, p. 52.

Arnold Print Works looms
Image courtesy of North Adams Historical Society

sion on Marshall Street. While David Brayton had supplied the necessary financial catalyst, ill health prevented him from adding much managerial support, and soon he had to cease his Fall River activities as well. He died in March 1882, forcing his son, David Jr., to return to Fall River to assume his father's duties. But by then Albert C. Houghton was already very much in charge, and the turnaround had been both quick and dramatic[16].

---

16   Cole, p. 62.

HOUGHTON IN CHARGE

—

By December 1879, all the feeder plants were running profitably, as was Arnold Print Works (APW), with annual sales of $2
million. Following David Brayton's death, Houghton gained full
control by buying out all the Brayton interests before embark-
ing on a major expansion on Marshall Street. By early 1893, ten
new buildings and their associated equipment had been added,
including two dye houses, a bleach house, color shop, drying
structure, and several warehouses. Then he built a new, integrated
Eclipse Mill, named after the Arnolds' original mill on Union
Street downstream from Beaver Mill. With the addition of this
mill, which employed all the necessary cotton cloth manufacturing processes, from carding to weaving, APW became completely
independent of non-captive sources of cotton cloth; Houghton's
vertical integration plan was complete. At the same time, Houghton began strengthening his sales activities by employing Faulk-
ner, Page & Co. to cover New York and Boston.

As APW prospered, Houghton's position in the community and
beyond continued to expand. He served as a trustee of Williams
College (1891–1910) and also of Boston College. He was a del-
egate to the Democratic National Convention in 1892 (he later
became a Republican) and was appointed commissioner of the
Chicago World's Fair in 1893; most importantly, he was elected North Adams's first mayor in 1896. Other directorships and
bank involvements followed. He continued to purchase property,
including a large parcel at the corner of Church and Pleasant
Streets where he built a beautiful residence just before the end of
the century. In a gesture that is one of his most enduring legacies,
in 1896 he purchased the Blackinton mansion at the corner of
Church and East Main and donated it to the city; it has served as

the North Adams Public Library since 1898. Still involved with land speculation, he and William A. Gallup, APW's treasurer, purchased Hathaway Farm, just northwest of the Marshall Street complex, to be subdivided into more than one-hundred building lots[17].

To date, APW had employed a number of different, but standard, direct printing processes, such as the use of madder in calico printing. This process produces what might be termed the fall colors—reds, browns, and yellows. But in 1883 Houghton gambled on something new and riskier, implementing the "blue dip" or indigo printing process to produce brilliant blues. Of the various approaches used in indigo printing, he chose so-called "reserve printing" because of its simplicity. Initially more expensive than direct dying (using engraved copper rollers for the blues as well as the other colors), Houghton felt, correctly, that in large volumes reserve printing would ultimately provide a lower cost.

Conceptually, reserve printing is similar to the technology used in manufacturing today's complex semiconductor devices, for which a silicon dioxide mask is used to provide protection for the material under it during a particular process. In "blue dip," the underlying cotton cloth is protected by a "reserve paste"—for example, a copper salt—while the rest of the material is dyed various shades of blue in the indigo vat. The paste is removed in an acid bath (similar to the silicon dioxide in semiconductors), and the previously protected white cotton cloth is dyed with other colors, using conventional techniques. The resulting trademarked Century Cloth came to dominate the worldwide textile printing industry. By 1883, five hundred workers in the Marshall Street factory, manning eight printing machines and two hundred

---

17   Cole, pp. 74, 75.

indigo vats, were producing this unique material at the rate of twenty thousand pieces a week. Houghton was also becoming a very wealthy man, although he continued to reinvest most of his money into the business[18].

The origin of printing patterns on cloth or other substances goes all the way back to antiquity, with some of the earliest examples found in China dating to 200 AD. The technique used a woodblock on which a pattern was carved; when the block was covered with a colorant and pressed on a substrate, only the color on the raised parts of the block was transferred, in the way a rubber stamp works. Multiple woodblocks used in sequence were employed to create complex multi-colored patterns. Textile printing began in England around 1676, but it wasn't until the latter part of the eighteenth century that Thomas Bell's roller printing patent, improved by Adam Parkinson in 1785, set the stage for the modern textile process using roller printing machines.

In such machines a rotating master cylinder has mounted copper rollers on its circumference, one for each color, on which are engraved that portion of the pattern which corresponds to each color. (APW had twenty-four machines, each capable of printing in twelve colors.) The fabric to be printed is pressed against the rotating master cylinder and its attached color rollers at high speeds, with everything aligned and synchronized so that in one complete rotation of the cylinder the entire pattern is printed. A drying and steaming cycle then fixes the colors. Printing speeds greater than one hundred yards per minute have been reported. The machines are huge, some as high as two stories, and alignment of the different parts of the equipment is obviously abso-

---

18   Cole, pp. 69–72.

lutely vital[19]. Because of the complexity, APW operators were required to serve a minimum seven-year apprenticeship.

Once a pattern specification was finalized, it went to the engraving department, where a sketch-maker transferred it to metal plates that could be used by pantograph operators to etch the pattern onto the copper printing rollers. Again, the apprenticeship was seven years, and at its peak the engraving department employed over seventy people. During APW's existence, this department engraved more than 69,000 patterns.

The key to success in the marketplace lay in the ability of a company to anticipate the current fashion needs of its customers and to be able to translate these needs into desired patterns and specifications. Similarly to today, the world's fashion centers were in New York and Paris, and fashion trends were tracked by Arnold offices in both locations[20].

By 1901, Houghton was spending most of his time in his New York headquarters on Leonard Street, concentrating on sales and marketing. Additional US field sales offices had also been opened in Boston, Chicago, St. Louis, Philadelphia, and Baltimore[21]. APW had additional offices around the world, employing close to thirty-three hundred in the North Adams facility and its subsidiary feeder plants, with the company and its captive material sources combining to form the largest and most successful textile

---

19 This is also true with complex silicon integrated circuits, in which the photolithographic masks for different parts of the process must be in perfect alignment.

20 *North Adams and Vicinity Illustrated*, p. 53.

21 *The Print Cloth Industry* (The Arnold and Windsor Print Works) (NA Historical Society, Inc., undated), pp. 1–3.

printing operation in the world. There were now twenty-six buildings on Marshall Street, covering ten acres, where more than a thousand workers used the world's most advanced textile printing equipment to produce 200,000 yards of dyed material a day for an annual revenue of $5 million. By 1906, this had increased to $9 million. Management began to believe this could go on forever[22].

As the chief executive officer of a successful entity, Houghton deservedly received the lion's share of the credit for what he had created. But APW was anything but a one-man organization. For example, he no longer ran the day-to-day operations, nor did he personally ever have the detailed knowledge and expertise to keep the company in a leadership position with the latest and most sophisticated manufacturing equipment. Complex chemical systems are required in multi-colored printing, and Houghton's success depended on his ability to surround himself with a world-class team of individuals who were specialists in all the facets of the business that were beyond his expertise. Besides William A. Gallup, his longest-tenured associate, there were a number of other key executives.

The Marshall Street plant was managed by R. L. Chase, an 1884 MIT graduate who, prior to joining APW in 1890 as head of one of its important new dying operations, had taught chemistry in Philadelphia at the Textile School. Chase's assistant was Dr. Arnold L. Bossi, a native of Italy with a portfolio of technical publications and multiple advanced degrees from Switzerland and London, who joined APW in 1903. The manager of the Beaver and Eclipse cotton cloth feeder plants was H. Burnham, who came to APW in the mid-1880s after gaining extensive textile

---

22   Cole, *Between Two Worlds*, pp. 75, 76.

manufacturing experience in several of the large eastern mills. R. R. Kelley was general superintendent, and George H. Flood had similar responsibility for the Williamstown and North Pownal operations (and later became a key manager at Sprague Specialties after it moved to North Adams in 1929).

Toward the end of the nineteenth century, the textile industry throughout the Northeast had begun to face severe competitive pressure from southern businesses with considerably lower wage structures and, in some cases, superior manufacturing capability. APW had been able to succeed because of its extremely efficient operations, continual reinvestment in property, plant, and equipment, being first to market with many new innovations, and just by sheer size. With ever-improving results, Houghton must have felt invincible. Not only was he running what many believed to be the most successful business of its kind in the world, he was also recognized as the leading citizen of the thriving city of North Adams, and people seemed to be reaching out to him for advice and involvement in an increasing breadth of activities.

Ever the gambler, in 1906 Houghton decided to improve the odds by taking the largest and, in hindsight, most disastrous risk of his life. Even though southern competition continued to intensify, and there were growing signs of a possible worldwide financial collapse, he attempted to corner the market by taking out huge loans and purchasing raw cotton far in excess of his short-term needs or, in fact, the needs of the entire Northeast textile industry. When the Panic of 1907 struck, industry production plummeted, and Houghton suddenly found himself with massive amounts of cotton he could neither use nor sell. Instead of the huge profits he had anticipated, he was now unable to pay off his loans as they matured. In effect, both he and APW were bankrupt, and Houghton faced the prospect of losing everything he had spent the last thirty years creating, while ripple effects devastated local employment and his beloved city[23].

Yet no one seemed to have the appetite to hold Houghton responsible for what happened, after all that he had accomplished in putting this small western Massachusetts city on the world map. Even today, the reasons for Arnold Print Works's demise are most often blamed on a combination of southern competition and a worldwide recession. After all, how could Houghton or anyone else have anticipated a world financial cataclysm? Regardless of the cause, APW, and therefore North Adams, were in deep trouble, with the plants forced to at least temporarily close. How to get them running again, as soon as possible and with Houghton still in charge, was the immediate problem.

A consortium of friendly creditors and receivers—including his nephew, Charles Houghton; brother-in-law, H. E. Werner; and good friend, Senator Murray Crane of Crane Paper—executed a patchwork of moves that, along with improved orders, opened APW again in early 1908, with Houghton still chief executive. But things were never the same. In 1908 and 1909, APW struggled to meet its city tax obligations. With no other choice, in 1910 Houghton started selling off the feeder plants, first the Beaver and Eclipse Mills (to a group from eastern Massachusetts, with William Butler of Butler Mills in New Bedford heading the new entity), and then the North Pownal and Williamstown mills (to William Plunkett of North Adams). At the time, Plunkett owned Greylock Mills Corporation, which will be revisited when discussing the role of Warren Buffett and Berkshire Hathaway.

---

23   Cole, pp. 75–78.

Despite failing health, Houghton continued to serve as president of APW. On August 1, 1914, he was riding in his new Pierce Arrow with a driver, his daughter Mary, and her friend Sybil Hutton, when a terrible accident killed both women. Although Houghton was only slightly injured, the driver committed suicide and, his spirit finally broken, Albert Charles Houghton died only a few days later, on August 11. It was a sad ending for a man who had accomplished so much[24].

It would seem logical that long-time treasurer, associate, and friend William A. Gallup would assume the presidency of APW after Houghton's death, and that is what Gallup's obituary reported in the August 11, 1930, issue of the North Adams Transcript. However, several issues of the APW newspaper The Arnold Print, which was published sporadically between 1918 and 1922, indicate otherwise. The December 19, 1919, issue recognized Gallup's long service as treasurer starting in 1883, while the July 1920 issue was dedicated to "our president" Darwin G. French, noting that French had joined the APW board in 1896 and had been named a vice president in 1913 and president in 1915, after Houghton's death. It can be speculated that the two men shared the company leadership, with Gallup perhaps in a role similar to chairman, chief executive officer, and treasurer, and French as president and chief operating officer. Whoever took the helm, APW's management was successful in guiding the company through the tumultuous years that followed, encompassing America's entry into World War I in 1917, the transition from a wartime to peacetime economy following the armistice, and much of the unstable Roaring Twenties. Arnold Print Works may have been wounded, but it was far from dead.

---

24   Cole, pp. 90, 91.

THE NEW ARNOLD PRINT WORKS
—

When the restructuring was finally completed in 1910 and
the feeder plants sold, Arnold Print Works was a much smaller
company, with perhaps a thousand employees. No longer ver-
tically integrated, in modern jargon—owning its own supply
chain—it had to operate with a very different business model.
Instead of purchasing its primary white cotton cloth material
from integrated feeder plants, cloth was received on consignment
from open-market suppliers and printed according to customer
specifications, a method that had already been the practice for
materials such as silk and rayon for many years. Business continued to improve, aided in no small part by military needs for cloth
when the United States finally joined the allies.

By the end of 1917, employment had grown to thirteen hundred, and business continued to improve until 1926, when APW
again became the dominant industrial manufacturer and largest
taxpayer in North Adams. This same year, Dr. Samuel M. Jones,
Gallup's son-in-law, took control of the business after all the
remaining interests of Gallup and the Houghton family had been
retired. A native of North Adams who had attended the town's
Drury High School, Dr. Jones returned to North Adams in 1915
to join APW as a chemist. Prior to this, he had received his PhD
in chemistry from the University of Basel in Switzerland, and
worked for the Zundel Print Works in Moscow, Russia, including
five years as general manager. At APW, he was named assistant
general manager of the Marshall Street plant in 1917 and general

manager in 1920[25].

Jones continued to grow the business, and, sensing a new opportunity to offset southern competitive pressure, in early 1929 he purchased and began to renovate the unused Renfrew Manufacturing Co. plant in Adams. Initially, this plant was to handle surplus orders, but it soon became a new business, exclusively manufacturing fine printed drapery material for such giants as Golding, Riverdale, Desley, Goldenheim, and Schumacher (the parent of Waverly Fabrics). This marked the division of APW into two separate and distinct businesses, with each taking a very different path. The so-called Jones Division, located in Adams, which would subsequently be sold several times, was able to stay in business until the early 1980s, long after the other parts of APW had disappeared and its empty buildings were housing diverse new tenants such as Sprague Electric. Over the years, when things looked bleakest, North Adams proved enormously flexible in responding to new business opportunities. This was undoubtedly the result of the ethnic diversity and broad mix of different skills of its population. If there is a theme to the history of 87 Marshall Street, it lies in this flexibility.

When the 1929 Great Depression struck, Arnold once more found itself in one of the ruinous down cycles that periodically plagued the industry. Textile firms and other businesses throughout the Northeast and the rest of the country were forced to shut down. Adding to the firm's woes, two years earlier a disastrous flood had destroyed much of the downtown section of North Adams. During the deluge the Marshall Street bridge had been torn from its footings and washed downstream until stopped by

---

25 *Historical Background of the Sprague Electric Plants (The Arnold Print Works, 1861–1943)* (North Adams Historical Society, Inc., undated), p. 5.

the Brown Street bridge, which luckily held fast. However, in the process, a seventy-five-foot section of the Marshall Street complex was ripped out. Just when it seemed things couldn't get any worse, APW workers went on strike, following a strong negative reaction to President Roosevelt's Depression-related "cotton textile code," which dictated textile printing workers' pay below what they had expected and felt they deserved, even as the recession worsened. It is not clear how long the walkout lasted or what effect it had on the firm, but, as seen later at Sprague Electric, such stoppages always have a strong negative impact on a company, especially during a recessionary period.

Despite all this, Jones proved to be an innovative manager, and, with a reduced workforce, lower wages, no bonuses, and other draconian cost-saving measures, APW continued to limp along with a greatly reduced work schedule. Even this wasn't enough, however, and on September 3, 1935, APW filed for Section 77B bankruptcy, and for the next two years operated under federal government control. As the world economy slowly began to recover, so did the textile industry, and the company went through one more period of prosperity. Reorganized once again and with Jones still at the helm, now free of extra-governmental controls, in January 1941 APW was able to declare its first dividend payment in more than eight years.

In a North Adams Historical Society publication on the history of APW, Mark Markarian (at the time a process development engineer at the Marshall Street plant who later worked in a similar capacity for Sprague Electric) describes in glowing terms APW's last hurrah in North Adams:

> *"The Arnold Print Works in North Adams, Massachusetts, during the period 1936–1942 was one of the largest textile*

dyeing and printing companies in the United States, second only to the Pacific Mills in Lawrence, Massachusetts, in size, output, and diversity of product. The Marshall Street physical plant covered approximately one million square feet, and there was also a smaller plant in Adams manufacturing very high-quality drapery material. In North Adams coal-fired furnaces provided energy for heating while electric motors ran the large machinery." [26]

World affairs once more intervened at Arnold Print Works. After the December 7, 1941, bombing of Pearl Harbor propelled the United States into World War II, civilian contracts dried up, as did the availability of textile cloth for non-military applications. Copper and the chemicals that had been used in the engraving operations were now required for the manufacture of artillery shells, and APW was unable to obtain any military contracts due in large part to competition from lower-cost southern factories. Seeing no other alternative, in 1942 the board of directors decided to liquidate the North Adams works. This was completed on November 18, 1943, after a two-day public auction, and the company that had served North Adams, the nation, and the world so well for eighty years was no more.

Fortunately for North Adams, the reverse was true for Sprague Electric, which was dealing with explosive growth. Sprague, which had moved from Quincy, Massachusetts, to North Adams in 1929, occupying first the former Arnold plant on Beaver Street and then the Brown Street plant, was desperate for added manpower and space. So Sprague quickly gobbled up the empty Marshall Street premises as well as much of the workforce, in-

---

26 Mark Markarian, *A Brief History of the Arnold Print Works* (North Adams Historial Society, undated), pp. 3, 4

cluding vital engineering and manufacturing talent. While there will be more to say about this in the chapters that follow, there is irony in the different impact of World War II on the two companies. While both the Civil War and World War I accelerated the growth of APW, World War II destroyed it. On the other hand, the contributions that Sprague Electric made to the war effort, both during and after World War II, were directly responsible for transforming what had been a fledgling capacitor manufacturer, whose primary market had been the US radio industry, into one of the world's largest and most successful electronic component suppliers.

It is difficult to understand why Arnold Print Works, with a rich history of survival, excellent management, and outstanding technical capability and manufacturing, was unable to successfully make the transition to a wartime economy. Competition from southern plants had been a long-term problem, and one wonders why APW hadn't already built, bought, or leased plants in lower labor-cost locations. In addition, there had been growing evidence throughout the 1930s that worldwide conflict that would radically change the market and affect the availability of crucial materials was inevitable. This should have provided a more than adequate lead time to inventory such materials—even if the need for fancy printed cloth was going to disappear, there was certainly going to be a market for millions of uniforms and other military cloth requirements. This need was going to be filled by United States firms, but not, as it turned out, by Arnold Print Works.

It was a different story in Adams, where the Jones drapery division of APW was somehow able to maintain very limited operations during the war and then resume growth during the 1950s, 1960s, and even early 1970s. This was due in large part to its well-deserved reputation as the high end "Tiffany" of the drapery printing industry. During this period it was sold several times, first to List Industries in 1953. By 1960, the president was North Adams native William J. Durocher and, along with a second plant in Hartsville, South Carolina, what had been the Jones Division of APW was now the textile division of the Glen Alden Corporation. Business was healthy, employment had reached seven hundred fifty people, annual payroll was $3 million, and the fourteen huge fourteen-color printers in the Adams Renfrew plant were capable of producing up to forty million yards of drapery and slipcover material a year[27]. However, as in the electronic components industry, worldwide competition continued to intensify, initially from lower-cost plants in the southern United States, and then from the Far and Middle East. The division was sold several more times, eventually to a group of local businessmen who tried desperately to keep it alive and maintain local employment. Nevertheless, competition eventually proved too strong, and when Waverly Fabrics, which had been renting storage space in Renfrew Mill, moved to the Carolinas, all was lost. Renfrew closed in 1983 and burned to the ground shortly afterwards, leaving only one building still standing. After a truly storied run, Arnold Print Works was finally dead.

In the meantime, Warren Buffett had come to town.

---

27   Sumner A. Keene, "Northern Berkshire Industries"
     (*North Adams Transcript*, 1960).

Greylock Mills
Photo by author

INTERLUDE: BERKSHIRE HATHAWAY

—

As noted, North Adams grew from a collection of sections or villages, most of which had one or more textile mills at their core. Examples include Blackinton, Braytonville, Beaver, and Union. Around each mill were different types of housing, one or more stores, and the inevitable church. One such area of North Adams is Greylock, where a two- or three-storied mill complex, comprising a number of interconnected wings, looms above the road as the traveler drives east from Williamstown into the city. Just east of the mill, there is housing, mostly to the right along Protection Avenue, Taft Street, and New Street, including several long buildings that must have once served as tenements. The Hoosic River winds under a bridge along Route 2 just east of New Street, much more peacefully now than when it was the major source of power for the mill. Just to the east of the river, Braytonville Village begins.

One house on Protection Avenue identifies itself as a Greylock Mill house (ca. 1890), while a housing section along Taft Street advertises itself as Spinning Mill Townhouses: "Stylish Berkshire Living at an Affordable Price." The housing is neat and well maintained, and one can easily imagine a time when this was a self-contained, thriving mill community. What makes this housing unique is its service as an early part of what eventually became Warren Buffett's wildly successful Berkshire Hathaway Corporation.

The first structure on the site was a single wooden building erected in 1804 as one of North Adams's earliest cotton mills. It was purchased in 1846 from David Temple by several of the North Adams McLellans and Hunters, after which there were a number of different owners until 1880, when a stock company was formed by Theodore Pomeroy of Pittsfield for the manufacture of ginghams. Around this same time, William Brown Plunkett of W. C. Plunkett & Sons became treasurer and manager of the Greylock Mills, and expansion began[28]. In 1889, Plunkett & Sons, with W. B. Plunkett having succeeded his father as senior partner, created the Berkshire Cotton Manufacturing Company in Adams, and by 1892 the Adams and Greylock mills had a combined total of some seventeen hundred workers and a capital base of $1,600,000.

World War I fueled continuing expansion, and in 1929 some half-dozen New England textile firms, including Berkshire Cotton Manufacturing and Greylock Mills, merged to form Berkshire Fine Spinning Associates, a combination which at the time accounted for nearly 25 percent of the United States' fine

---

28   Spear, *History of North Adams*, p. 82.

cotton textile production. Berkshire Fine Spinning survived the Great Depression, but market factors and southern competition took their toll, although, unlike Arnold Print Works, demand was briefly increased by military clothing requirements during World War II and the Korean conflict that followed. Nevertheless, it was clear that some sort of industry consolidation was necessary, and in 1955 Berkshire Fine Spinning merged with New Bedford-based textile manufacturer Hathaway Manufacturing Company to form Berkshire Hathaway, Inc.[29] The new company had too many plants, more than six million square feet, some ten thousand workers, and, not surprisingly, miserable financial performance. It was immediately clear to the new management team that drastic cost reductions were required, and the northern Berkshire facilities were among the first to be axed.

Shortly after the merger, in 1956, Berkshire Hathaway closed the Greylock Mills and moved production to Adams. The resultant euphoria in Adams was short-lived, being quickly replaced by the same shock, anger, and frustration felt in Greylock when only two years later Berkshire Hathaway announced closure of the Adams mill complex, ending one hundred fifty years of textile manufacturing in the Berkshires and forfeiting one thousand jobs in Adams[30].

This was only the beginning, however, as the company continued further consolidations and plant closings right into the 1960s. Then 1965 brought a radical change in management, when a partnership headed by Warren Buffett, a then-obscure investor

---

29 Berkshire Fine Spinning Associates, http://en.wikipedia.org/wiki/Berkshire_Fine_Spinning_Associates

30 *North Adams Transcript*, May 7, 1958.

MASS MoCA main entrance and *Tree Logic*
Photo: Zoran Orlic

Don Gummer sculpture, *Primary Separation*, at former Sprague Electric Research Center.
Photo: Elizabeth Berg

Installation view of *Simon Starling: The Nanjing Particles*, 2008
Photo: Arthur Evans

Joseph Beuys
Lightning with Stag in Its Glare
Photo: Nicholas Whitman

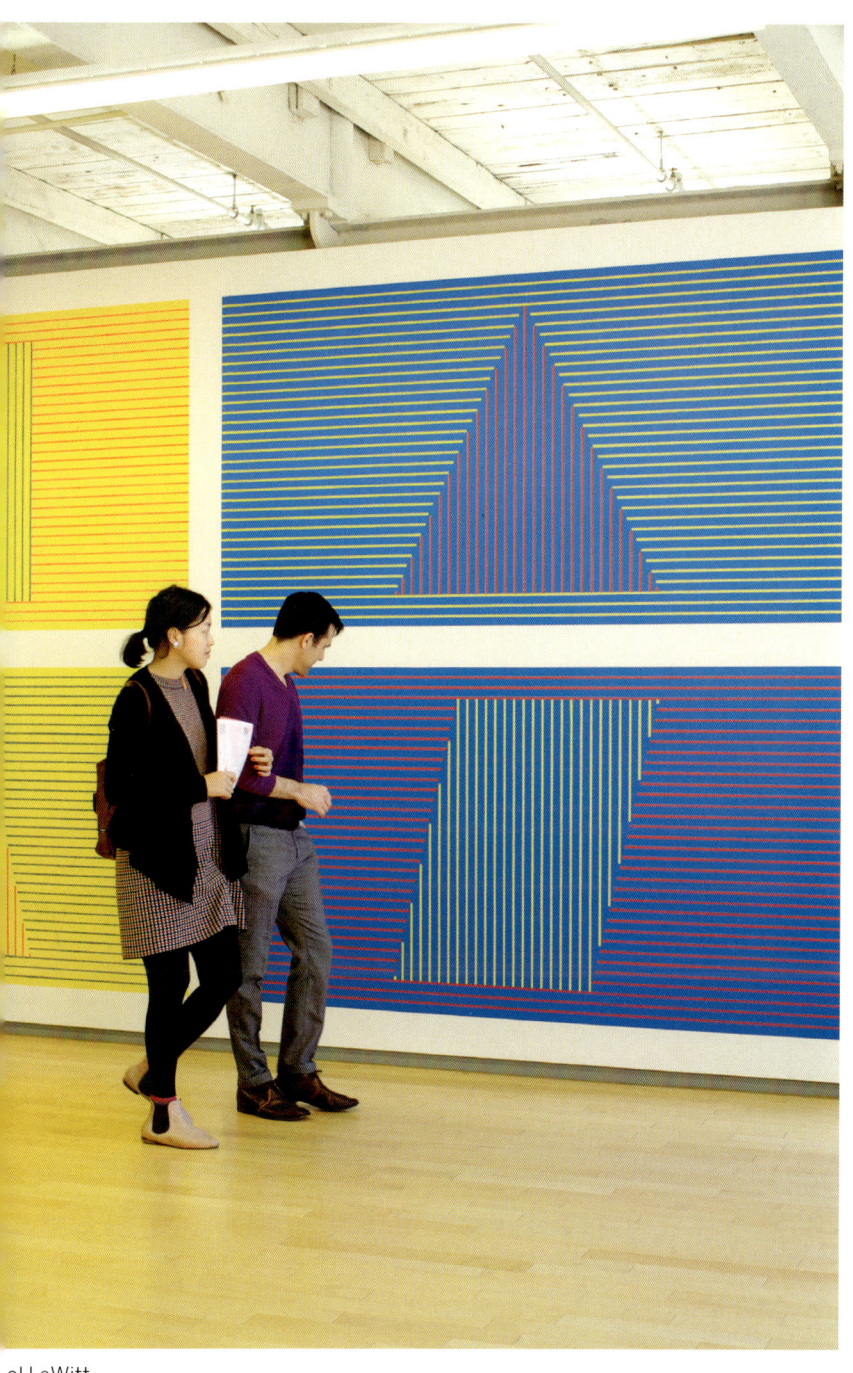

ol LeWitt
Wall Drawing 340, 1980 (Detail)
Photo: Zoran Orlic

Vaughn Bell
Village Green, 2008
Photo: Kevin Kennefick

Installation of *Mike Kelly* by Jennifer Steinkamp in Building #4 in the exhibition
Badlands: New Horizons in Landscape from May 24, 2008 to April 12, 2009
Photo: Kevin Kennefick

Anselm Kiefer
Etroits sont les Vaisseaux, 2002, concrete, steel, lead and earth
Photo: Kevin Kenneflck

based in Omaha, Nebraska, purchased enough stock to take control. Buffett had started buying shares in 1962, not to purchase the company, but because the shares were cheap and he believed he could make a sizeable profit when Berkshire Hathaway chief executive officer Seabury Stanton, who was obsessed with maintaining control, bought them back at a higher price. Then Stanton reneged on a handshake deal between the two men. Furious, Buffett vowed to gain control and oust the man who had tried to outwit him. It had little to do with the value of the business and much to do with personal pride. When Buffett finally won control in 1965 and became chairman, he claimed he had received a fair price. Later he would admit that buying Berkshire Hathaway was the worst mistake in his illustrious career. Still, he initially tried to make a go of it, and changes in top management, along with cost-cutting, led to small profits in 1965 and 1966.

The headquarters were gradually moved from New Bedford, Massachusetts, to Omaha, and when financial hemorrhaging renewed in 1967, Buffett countered the textile industry's deteriorating fundamentals and cyclicality by initiating a major diversification effort, starting with the acquisition of the National Indemnity Company, several other insurance companies, and Sun Newspapers. Buffett proved to be an investment genius with a now-famous long-term outlook, and over time was able to transform a dying textile company into one of the most successful diversified financial holdings in the world. He did try to make viable, for as long as possible, what remained of core textile businesses; it wasn't until 1985, with no interested buyer, those operations were finally liquidated[31].

---

31   Alice Schroeder, *The Snowball: Warren Buffett and the Business of Life* (New York: Bantam Dell, Division of Random House, 2008).

It was a noble effort: By this time, even electronic component manufacturing in northeastern cities, such as North Adams, was facing possible extinction.

CHAPTER FOUR

SPRAGUE SPECIALTIES COMPANY (1926–1945)

CREATION, DEPRESSION, AND WORLD WAR II
—

The story of Sprague Electric Company begins in 1926 in Quincy, Massachusetts. There, working part-time in their kitchen, a young couple named Robert C. (R.C.) and Florence Sprague built by hand the first product of a business that grew into one of the world's leading electronic component manufacturers. Initially named Sprague Specialties, it soon outgrew its Quincy location. Moving to North Adams in 1929 to enable the expansion of the growing business, it occupied 87 Marshall Street during World War II, and, like Arnold Print Works before it, eventually dominated the local economy. Sprague's world superiority in passive electronic components began to fade in the 1970s, and by 1990 it had been acquired twice and disappeared as an entity.

However, the Sprague Electric Company, founded by Robert C. Sprague, wasn't the first to hold the family name. That distinction belonged to a company established by his father, electrical

Frank J. Sprague at 75
Photo courtesy of author

inventor Frank J. Sprague, who coincidentally spent his boyhood in North Adams and was undoubtedly the genetic source of the skills of his three sons: Desmond, Robert, and Julian. He had considerable influence on all three, but often in ways more subtle than obvious.

FRANK JULIAN SPRAGUE

—

Frank Julian Sprague was born in 1857 in Milford, Connecticut, but grew up in North Adams, where he lived with a maiden aunt after the death of his mother in 1866 and his father's departure to seek his fortune in the west. Frank attended Drury Academy in North Adams and then the US Naval Academy, graduating in 1878 with honors in math and science. Following active duty, he worked for eleven months for Thomas Edison before forming the Sprague Electric Railway and Motor Company (SERM). SERM was a pioneer in electric motors and in 1888 completed the world's first commercial electrification of a street railway system, in Richmond, Virginia.

After selling SERM to Edison General Electric (later GE) in 1889, Frank Sprague formed the Sprague Electric Elevator Company (SEEC) with Charles W. Pratt. SEEC pioneered elevator electrification in New York's new fourteen-story Postal Telegraph Building. During the installation, Sprague intuited a system for simultaneously controlling six elevators from a single location. Later, this became his most important invention, the multiple unit control system (MU) that revolutionized urban railway and subway systems worldwide, and it is still widely used today.

MU was first commercialized in Chicago in 1887, and after selling SEEC to Otis, in 1898 Sprague formed the Sprague Electric

Company (SEC) to commercialize the invention. Following bitter patent litigation with GE, the Sprague patent prevailed, and in 1902 GE purchased SEC, making Frank J. Sprague a wealthy man.

Far from retiring, in 1902 Sprague became a key member of the Electric Traction Commission, managing the electrification of Grand Central Station, and during World War I served with distinction on the Naval Consulting Board chaired by Thomas Edison.

Despite later ventures—such as the Sprague Safety Control and Signal Corporation and Sprague Sign Company—being commercial failures, when Frank Sprague died in 1934 he was widely revered as the "Father of Electric Traction."

Married twice and the father of four, Frank J. Sprague saw two of his three sons, Robert C. and Julian, become active in what was the second Sprague Electric Company, followed by Robert C.'s two sons, Robert Jr. and John[1].

ROBERT CHAPMAN (R.C.) SPRAGUE
—

Robert C. (R.C.) Sprague was born in New York City on August 3, 1900. There is little information on his early life except what was gleaned in an extraordinary interview that author John L. Sprague's youngest son, David, conducted with his grandfather when he was a student at Williams College[2]. In this interview

---

1   For more on Frank J. Sprague see Frank Rowsome, Jr., The Birth of Electric Traction, the Extraordinary Life and Times of Inventor Frank Julian Sprague, (IEEE History Center Press, 2013)

2   Robert C. Sprague, interviewed by his grandson, David Sprague, 1985; author's personal papers.

R.C. talks about his early years, about meeting David's grand-mother, and about his extensive involvement with the US government, starting in 1952.

JOHN L. SPRAGUE RECALLS: *My father was in his late eighties during much of David's interview, and the details he was able to recall at that age are amazing. However, he refused to talk about Sprague Electric. I don't know if he was embarrassed by the ultimate demise of the company he had founded and run for so many years, or if it was part of a past in which he had no further interest.*

R.C. BEGINS, "Originally I went to the Collegiate School in New York, which was a very fine private school close to where we lived on 71st Street. Then my family sent me away for a year to the Curtiss School. It wasn't a good experience because of its demerit system which involved crushing rock. When my father came down to bring me home at the end of the school year, he had to stay an extra day for me to work off my demerits and my hands were pretty well bloodied from broken blisters. He didn't think it was an appropriate school from which to get an education. Neither did I.

"I went to Hotchkiss, Class of 1918, as a sophomore (I don't think they were called sophomores then), and at that time if you were a Hotchkiss boy you were supposed to go to Yale. But the world situation was fairly ominous, and my father talked about the possibility of my going to the Naval Academy instead. He was able to get me an appointment provided I could pass an exam, and I did. So I left Hotchkiss during my junior year and went to the Naval Academy when I was only sixteen. I entered as a member of the Class of 1921A, but because of the war in Europe we were accelerated to graduate in 1920 [hence the A]. Then, because of my high grades, I was accelerated another year and actually graduated in 1919 at the age of nineteen."

JLS: *R.C. always seemed to take this progression for granted, although graduating from the US Naval Academy at the age of nineteen was no small feat.*

When asked how he was influenced by his father, R.C. replied, "When I was growing up he had been a leader in the electrical industry for twenty-five years, and I wasn't very conscious of this. Certainly in my early days I wasn't impressed with the fact that he was considered world-wide as a genius in this area. He was just my father. But he did have an experimental machine shop in New York and I spent a great deal of time down there learning how to use some of the tools, like lathes."

JLS: *My father's feelings about his father were ambivalent. He recognized that he was an inventive genius, but faulted him as a businessman who died nearly penniless after running through several small fortunes.*

When David asked his grandfather how Sprague Specialties got started, instead of an answer he got a rambling discourse describing his sea duty experiences and how he met David's grandmother ("Mimi" to her grandchildren). The parents of Florence van Zelm had a summer home on Twin Lakes, Connecticut, some fifteen miles from the Frank Sprague home in Sharon, Connecticut, and R.C.'s Hotchkiss roommate, Bob Lesher, had dated her. She was described glowingly as a wonderful dancer and "just about the most attractive girl" at a Hotchkiss dance that R.C. had not attended. He fretted about how he could meet her until his younger brother, Julian, said, "Why don't you just call her?" So he did, using the ruse that they had met at the Hotchkiss dance, when, of course, they hadn't. Initially, she responded coolly, but encouraged by her mother, a wonderfully loving and engaging woman, she invited him to visit the following day. He arrived in full dress Navy whites, white gloves and all, driving a modified Pierce Arrow 66. True to form, he would brag later, "She never had a chance!" But anyone knowing "the van Zelm girl" would believe just the opposite was true. Regardless, it was that afternoon that the romance that would last for sixty-seven years began.

The family of Florence's mother, born Antoinette Gray Hyatt and known as "Nettie," was among the early settlers of New England. She cared only about her daughter's happiness and encouraged the relationship. But her father was another matter. Johannes Louis van Zelm was born in Rotterdam, the Netherlands, and moved to the United States when he was four. While he was a vice president of the New York Life Insurance and Trust Company (later the Bank of New York & Trust Company) when R.C. and Florence met, van Zelm was also serving the Netherlands in various capacities (in 1938 he was awarded the Officers' Cross of the Order of the Orange-Nassau by Queen Wilhelmina). Much colder and more austere in appearance than actuality, he adored his daughter and initially was violently opposed to R.C. as a suitor: "Just another sailor with a girl in every port." He even went so far as to hire a private detective to try and determine, apparently unsuccessfully, that Ensign Sprague was untrustworthy.

Shortly after they met, R.C. left for his first cruise as a Junior Engineering Officer on the battleship USS Pennsylvania, which took him to Havana and then through the Panama Canal to Lima, Peru. While he was gone, he and Florence wrote letters to each other almost daily, and it soon became apparent that they wanted to get married as rapidly as possible after the fleet returned. Since her father was still opposed to having the young couple even see

Ensign Robert C. and Florence A. Sprague
Photo courtesy of author

each other, Ensign Sprague took control. "I finally went to see him at the bank and told him, as nicely as possible, that whether he liked it or not, we were going to get married, and we hoped that he and Mrs. van Zelm would come to the wedding. Faced with the inevitable, Florence's father finally relented, and since then my relations with him couldn't have been better."
Florence Antoinette van Zelm and Ensign Robert Chapman Sprague were married on May 24, 1921, following which he attended the US Naval Postgraduate School, receiving a BS degree in engineering in 1922. Having decided to switch from a career as a general sea duty line officer to naval architecture, R.C. went to MIT, where he earned an MS in 1924. Then he joined the staff supervising the design and construction of the aircraft carrier USS Lexington in the Charlestown Naval Shipyard. The young couple settled in Quincy, Massachusetts, where they would live for the next six years, during which time the Sprague Specialties Co. would be formed, R.C. would resign from the Navy (in 1928), and Robert Chapman Sprague Jr. and John Louis Sprague, the author of this narrative, would be born. Barely in their twenties when this odyssey began, R.C. and Florence were an extraordinary young couple.

Van Zelm family photographs show Florence as a lovely, slim young woman with an oval face, bobbed brown hair, and blue-grey eyes that seem to look right into the soul. In every photograph, she has a serious expression—except for one in which she flashes a blazing smile in R.C.'s direction. Throughout her life, this seemingly reserved woman hid a fun-loving streak as well as an iron will, both of which she would need in the years ahead. She never went to college but studied both piano and voice at the New York Conservatory of Music and continued with the piano at the New England Conservatory of Music. She continued to play complex classical piano for many years, until arthritic hands made that impossible. While living in Quincy in the 1920s she was active in the theater, and in 1983 was cited by Governor Michael Dukakis for her "unflagging dedication to the cultural community of the Commonwealth."[3] In many ways she was a match for, and necessary complement to, her husband. In the same photograph, he appears to be of medium height, sturdy, and well built (he was a good athlete throughout his life and still skiing in his eighties); handsome in his Navy blues he smiles broadly at his wife, his square face dominated by a slightly curved nose. Behind the crinkled eyes lurks a certain aura of authority—no matter what R.C. became involved in, he inevitably ended up in charge.

SPRAGUE SPECIALTIES COMPANY

—

Grandson David Sprague was unable to learn how the Sprague Specialties Company was formed, so just how did it happen? His grandfather's own words explain it best, from a presentation on Sprague Electric in North Adams made in Boston on November 6, 1958, to the Newcomen Society in North America. (In 1943, the name was changed from Sprague Specialties to Sprague Electric, the title of his father, Frank J. Sprague's, most important company.) Accompanying R.C. at this presentation were a whopping twenty of his key managers and directors, for Sprague Electric was on a roll. R.C. writes in the Newcomen press release: "[Compared] to the original work force of two in the Sprague home in 1926, there are now more than 5,000 [in plants around the world], and what was originally a single product has grown to products with more than 40,000 different specifications and sales of $46,000,000."

---

3   Author's personal papers.

Quincy Sprague Specialties Headquarters, circa 1927
Photo courtesy of author

R.C. CONTINUED, "The story of Sprague Electric began in Quincy, Massachusetts, in 1925 with the invention of a Tone Control device." In the 1920s, radios were all the rage, but the young ensign didn't like the sound of his and started to experiment with methods of improving it using a group of condensers (now called capacitors) of different values to vary the tone of the radio. The result was a tapped fixed paper condenser, of a completely new design, and an accompanying switch that could be used to choose seven different capacity values between the output of the radio circuitry and the speaker and therefore vary the tone. People who heard the result felt it greatly improved the performance of the radio and suggested that a business could be built around it. So in early 1925 a series of patents was filed on the device, as well as the unique condenser that was its heart, and "Tone Control" was registered with the US Patent Office.

A little over a year later, in June 1926, the Sprague Specialties Company was incorporated with an initial capitalization of $25,000, of which $3,200 came from R.C. and Florence's personal savings. Since Ensign Robert Sprague was still on active duty in the Charlestown Navy Yard, Sprague Specialties was strictly a moonlighting operation. Everything was accomplished by the two unpaid employees in their Quincy home, first in the kitchen and then in the basement. It is unlikely Florence Sprague had expected that, in her mid-twenties, she would be simultaneously supporting a husband who was working two jobs, bringing up a young child (Robert C. Sprague Jr. was born in 1922), doing most of the paperwork for a nascent company and, in her spare time, helping to manufacture a strange thing called a condenser. She was relieved of the paperwork aspect of her job when the company's first paid employee, Miss Mary E. ("Molly") Avery joined them and assumed responsibility for correspondence, bookkeeping, and other clerical work. Molly also became personal secretary to R.C., a position she held for the next thirty-five years. Although the original plan had been to subcontract the manufacture of the condensers and their assembly into the Tone Control, as well as promotion and sales, "that didn't work out as planned, and we had to take over both manufacturing and sales, without any experience in either!" Even worse, no one seemed interested in purchasing the finished device, and by mid-November 1926 more than half of the miniscule seed capital was gone.

R.C. Sprague's younger brother, Julian, had joined the firm

shortly after it was formed. His title was production manager, although like everyone else he was initially a jack-of-all-trades. Despite lacking his brother's formal engineering background and training, he was certainly bright and made a significant early contribution when he concluded that the key asset owned by the company was the heart of the Tone Control, the small tapped paper condenser. He suggested making a single fixed condenser using the same basic paper/metal film construction as the multi-position unit. The resulting "Midget" was half the size and one eighth the weight of the standard mica condenser then in use and offered by such established giants as Cornell Dubilier. It also had nearly equivalent electrical and life performance and, because of the method of construction and materials used, was much less expensive to manufacture. Following Julian's suggestion, the Tone Control was shelved and, using what was left of the initial capital, the company bet its future on the "Midget," much as Frank J. Sprague had done in the majority of his ventures.

Just what is a condenser or capacitor? (Capacitor, the more modern term, will be used from now on). Conceptually, it is an extremely simple device in which two, generally metal conductors are separated by an insulator (dielectric): for example, paper or a synthetic film such as Mylar, mica, metal oxides of aluminum or tantalum, or ceramic materials, or even air. It is used to store energy and blocks the flow of direct current (DC) while passing alternating current (AC). The first such device was a "Leyden Jar" developed independently in 1745 in Germany and Holland and a year later in England by John Bevis. Because of the initial construction (a glass jar surrounded by two pressed metal conductors) its ability to store electric charge or capacitance was extremely low. The electric energy storage capability for a parallel plate capacitor can be calculated as follows:

$$C = K'K\ A/D$$

where K' is a dimensioned constant, K is the dimensionless dielectric constant of the insulator, A is the area of the conducting plates, and d is the thickness of the insulator

The manufacturer wants a high K, lots of area, and as thin a dielectric as possible, as long as it still has satisfactory breakdown strength (so a short circuit won't occur in the dielectric under the voltage used in the application). C is most often expressed in microfarads (10^{-6} F) or nanofarads (10^{-9} F). Over the years, some very exotic materials and construction techniques have been developed to satisfy these requirements, many of them by Sprague Electric.

Commercial use of capacitors began in the late 1800s, first in telegraphy, then telephony, and finally radio. Today they are utilized everywhere. The use of stacked cleaved mica as a dielectric was first demonstrated in 1845, while early work on aluminum electrolytic capacitors began nine years later[4]. The superiority of the Midget was due to much less expensive materials and construction (rolled metal film and paper versus stacked metal film and cleaved mica) and a considerably thinner dielectric.

Sprague sent samples and promotional materials to radio manufacturers, and the response was immediate and positive. Why wouldn't they want a competitive device that was not only much smaller and lighter, but also much less expensive? Despite some concern about the long-term viability of an untested new company, orders began to pour in, and the tiny firm had to immediately

---

4   For more details on how a capacitor is manufactured and used, see John L. Sprague, *Revitalizing US Electronics, Lessons from Japan* (Stoneham, MA: Butterworth-Heinemann, 1993).

scramble for additional manufacturing space, new machinery, and production workers. Sprague Specialties was off to the races.

Returning to the Newcomen presentation, "Sales in 1927 were $54,000 as against almost nothing the year before, and increased to $234,000 in 1928 with a net profit of $35,000. By the time it neared its third birthday in 1929, Sprague's employment had risen from the original two persons to a peak of 550 and its sales were running in excess of half a million dollars."

R.C. was both president and treasurer, but he was no longer working alone, and early board of directors minutes and annual reports provide a hint about how the company evolved[3]. In March 1927, Sprague Specialties was located at 1511 Hancock Street in Quincy. William J. Nolan, who became a close confidant to R.C., was clerk; until his death in 1974 he was the company's chief counsel and a member of the board. Harry Kalker was also one of the earliest employees, joining the company in 1926. He formed Sprague Products in 1933 to handle "consumer sales" of small orders to, for example, radio parts jobbers who used Sprague capacitors to repair radio sets. Over the years, such retail sales grew to account for nearly one-third of Sprague's electronic component sales.

Although he could probably ill afford it, another early stockholder was Frank J. Sprague. While it appears that he exerted no direct influence on the running of the company, and attended meetings only by proxy, his presence must certainly have been felt. By 1933, all three of his sons and his son-in-law were employed by Sprague Specialties. Desmond was the oldest son, but with the failure of his father's last two companies , it was R.C. Sprague who had assumed responsibility for trying to help his siblings in any way he could. When Desmond joined in 1929

Frank J. Sprague family, 1932. Standing left to right: Helene and Julian, Robert C. (Florence is absent), Desmond and Ruth, Bud Tucker; seated: Harriet, Frank J. Sprague, Althea Sprague Tucker.
Photo courtesy of author

as plant engineer, he had been without a job, and we can only assume the same of Bud Tucker, the husband of R.C. and Julian's sister Althea, who joined the sales force in 1933 at the height of the Depression. R.C. later vowed that he would never allow his family to face the same type of financial difficulties he did after the death of his father.

In addition to R.C. and Bill Nolan, William R. Hurley, H. Fred

Lalley, and Julian K. Sprague were early elected directors. Over the next several years, both Hurley and Julian became vice presidents. Capitalization was increased in April 1928 and regularly thereafter. In March 1929, the president's salary was set at $7,500 annually. Just three weeks before "Black Friday" (October 18, 1929), when the New York Stock Exchange began its precipitous collapse, Sprague Specialties purchased Beaver Mills from the North Adams Industrial Company for $42,000 with funds "derived from the sale of blocks of preferred and common stock to North Adams individuals. Extensive credit to finance the move and provide additional capital was obtained from Boston and North Adams banks." In addition to the new plant, at the 1929 annual meeting (held March 3, 1930) there seemed only good news to report: earnings of $73,899 (before taxes, depreciation, and reserves) on sales of $576,534; net worth of $492,282; and a brand new aluminum electrolytic product line[5]. Revenues for 1930 were forecast to exceed $1 million, and there were "important new management additions in Sales, Engineering, Operations, and Research." In light of what was happening in the world economy at that time, today it seems impossible to understand such a rosy outlook, but as R.C. said, "We were young, optimistic, and certain that we had what it took to run a business."[6] So, apparently, were the investors.

In 1929, two key management additions helped enhance the future of the emerging company. After four years in ship construc-

---

5   An electrolytic capacitor has one conducting plate or anode, usually very high-purity aluminum or tantalum, on which a thin metal oxide is formed as the dielectric and a conducting electrolyte (which can be a liquid, "dry," or "solid") for electrical connection to the cathode, which is often a metal can. The "dry" aluminum electrolytic capacitor was licensed in the early 1930s from P. R. Mallory, a Sprague competitor, under its Sam Ruben patents.

6   Robert C. Sprague interview, 1985.

tion at the Portsmouth Navy Yard, Carleton Shugg, a brilliant former naval officer and classmate of R.C. at both Annapolis and MIT, was hired as production manager and given complete responsibility for bringing Beaver Mills into production. Shugg served in that capacity until late 1940 when, feeling he could best serve his country by returning to shipbuilding, he resigned to join the Cramp Shipbuilding Company in Philadelphia. Shugg had a remarkable career. After several more shipbuilding jobs he moved on to the Atomic Energy Commission[7], eventually becoming its general manager, where he hired Hyman Rickover to lead the nuclear propulsion program. In 1951, he joined the Electric Boat Division of General Dynamics and soon became division president. While there, he and Rickover began to build the nation's fleet of nuclear submarines and, in the late 1950s, with Admiral William Raborn, the first missile-equipped submarines. He retired in 1965 and lived until 1992.

JOHN L. SPRAGUE RECALLS: *Although Carl was still a young man when he was at Sprague Specialties, he was my father's closest confidant. I remember him being a short, powerfully built, unsmiling man with a seemingly encyclopedic understanding of how to manufacture almost anything—an individual who always said exactly what he believed, regardless of the consequences.*

Throughout his business career, R.C. always emphasized research and development as the best way to continually feed the company with a portfolio of new products. Two major new developments (the most noteworthy of which was the aluminum electrolytic capacitor) introduced in 1929 helped save the company from

---

7   *North Adams Transcript*, August 9, 1948.

Dr. Preston Robinson, circa 1950
Photo courtesy of author

almost certain bankruptcy. In 1929, Dr. Preston Robinson was hired to formalize and staff Sprague Specialties' first research and development department. Dr. Robinson grew up in Brookline, Massachusetts, and received his BS in 1922 and MS in 1923, both from MIT, and his PhD from the University of California in 1925. He returned east to work in the Guggenheim Research Laboratories, where he met Frank J. Sprague and soon afterward joined Sprague Specialties in Quincy as chief technical officer. He was then elected vice president for research and engineering, and in 1932 joined the board of directors, a position he maintained until 1967. In 1953, his administrative responsibilities were assumed by Dr. Wilbur Lazier, and he became a senior technical consultant, a position he held for the rest of his life. Measured by number of patents, Robinson was Sprague's most prolific scientist with 114 US patents, the most important of which was the basic patent for the solid-electrolyte capacitor. On May 25, 1965, he received special recognition for receipt of Sprague Electric's five hundredth patent. Still filing patents in his late sixties, he died in 1973[8].

NORTH ADAMS

—

The October 3, 1929, *North Adams Transcript* trumpeted, "Electrical Industry Employing 1,000 to Locate Here; Sprague Specialties Co. of Quincy, Massachusetts, Selects North Adams in Which to Expand; Beaver Mills Bought; $100,000 Is Raised by Business Men of North Adams." The article continued with a brief history of the company and a description of the competitive battle with other Massachusetts cities such as Lowell and Holyoke,

---

8 *North Adams Transcript*, May 23, 1973.

and was linked to a long accompanying item about Frank J. Sprague. But why move at all, and why was North Adams finally chosen? There were two problems in Quincy. First there just wasn't enough building room for the anticipated level of employment. Secondly, the existing space was in violation of the local sanitation laws, and the addition of the required extra toilets would require expensive renovation. So the company headed to North Adams, where Frank J. Sprague had grown up.

JLS: *In a private conversation many years later, my father told a more interesting story: "After considering locating in some of the larger metropolitan areas around Boston, we decided we should also look at the far western part of the state where we had heard there was plenty of available factory space and labor in Adams. So the two of us took Route 2 over the Mohawk Trail and arrived in North Adams in the early afternoon. Unable to find any road signs to Adams, we asked directions from a man standing on a corner. Looking us over carefully, he asked why we wanted to go there. On learning the reason for the trip, the man (believed to be either Frank Bond or George B. Flood) declared, 'Hey, you don't need to go to Adams; we have everything you need right here in North Adams.' And the rest is history."*

Returning to the Newcomen talk: "The North Adams renovated plant began operations on April 1, 1930 (with some twenty-five young women who had been through a two-week training program), and by mid-year employment reached 200, and was forecast to reach 600 to 700 by year-end 1930. In June 1931, the sales office and "experimental laboratory" moved from Quincy to Beaver Street in North Adams, and the Sprague Company had become a 100 percent local North Adams industry. "At the end of 1930 our optimism seemed justified. Sales had increased almost

50 percent over 1929, although we were beginning to see a disturbing downward trend in the ratio of net profit over sales. Next year, we told ourselves, we will tighten up." An impressive 1929 list of customers included Burroughs, Columbia Radio Corp., GE, Magnavox, Raytheon, and Westinghouse. Soon Philco would be added to the list and become Sprague's largest customer.

July 1931 saw the introduction of an unusual invention by R.C. and his brother, Julian. Called the Visivox, it was a complete home entertainment system that included a 16mm movie projector, a synchronized record player, an amplifier/radio, and a built-in speaker. There were even plans for a circulating film library. However, the project was quickly dropped due to the highly negative reaction of some of Sprague's customers, especially Philco, which objected to having one of its component suppliers as a competitor. Today, one of the few surviving Visivox models is often on display in the MASS MoCA lobby at 87 Marshall Street.

In 1931 sales exceeded $1 million for the first time, but, soon after, the roof fell in. Despite record sales, expenses were out of control; as R.C. stated in his Newcomen speech, "our informal management systems had broken down and our expenditures were significantly above our receipts, [causing] a net loss of truly staggering proportions [$295,000 on sales of $1,175,000]."

Continuing at Newcomen, R.C. candidly described how this could have happened. "Most of the new research-based enterprises in New England, such as Sprague Specialties, were created and operated by people with scientific and technical, rather than general, business backgrounds. In 1930 most of our business experience was limited to supplying a product greatly in demand by a market which seemed to be growing by geometric progression. So the New York consulting firm of Stevenson, Jordan & Harrison was brought in to not only modernize the company's accounting and operational controls, but also to study plant layout and compensation systems. Inventories were slashed and, among other draconian measures, all product and process research was temporarily eliminated as well as any new equipment and facilities expenditures."

The company also needed to obtain at least two-year extensions on their loans from banks and other major creditors. Here, vital local help came to the rescue. At the request of the bank creditors, George B. Flood joined the company to look at its finances, first without pay as an informal observer, and then as full-time treasurer, replacing R.C. With extensive prior business experience as treasurer of Arnold Print Works, he became a key member of the management team and would remain at Sprague in that capacity until 1953, when R.C. again assumed the treasurer's role. Flood's son-in-law, Neal Welch, joined the sales organization in 1932, initially working in inside sales. Rising through the organization, he first succeeded Julian Sprague as vice president of sales after his untimely death in 1960, and then followed R.C. as CEO in 1971.

The rigid cost controls worked, at least as far as short-term financial stability was concerned, although in the process long-term viability was severely threatened. Even though 1932 sales were only $671,000 (57 percent of the prior year) the loss dropped (to $32,800), and from then on, despite a number of economic cycles in between, the company had an enviable record of continuous profitability until 1968. By 1936, not only had Sprague Specialties survived, it had paid off nearly all of its $800,000 deferred liabilities, had nearly $250,000 cash in the bank, and reported record sales of $2,902,000 and profits of $284,000. In early February 1937, the company purchased the former Hoosac

Worsted Mill plant on Brown Street in North Adams for both protection and further expansion.

Between 1933 and 1936 sales had nearly tripled, but this was mostly due to new products that had been developed prior to 1932. Further new product development stopped in 1932, and the results of this were about to be felt. Product life cycles vary widely, but the gestation period for a truly new product from research to billable sales can easily exceed three years or more. With a greatly improved financial base, in 1936 Sprague had reactivated its dormant research and development activities and begun to hire an extremely competent group of scientists and engineers to rebuild its laboratories. But the results of this effort would not begin to appear until the end of the decade, just in time to respond to Pearl Harbor.

During the Depression, all of Sprague's competitors, such as Cornell Dubilier and P. R. Mallory Co., had also curtailed expenses, but their R&D budgets had not been reduced to the same extent as that of Sprague Specialties. R.C. stated, "By 1937 competition was finding ways of equaling or improving much of what we had to sell. Whipsawed by competition on old products and stymied by the laboratory-to-production time lag on new ones [despite an impressive customer base that included Philco, Delco Radio, Emerson Electric, Ford Motor Company, and Westinghouse], our 1938 sales were only two-thirds of those for 1936 and profits had slipped from 11 to under 3 percent." It would take new products and a wartime economy to turn the tide.

Another factor proved critical when Sprague Specialties moved into the defense sector. Since its formation, the company had developed a well-earned reputation for superior quality and reliability. For example, during a mid-1930s sales call to Philco, R.C. sat quietly in front of the purchasing manager as his competitors gave their pitches with their products lined up on the desktop blotter. The capacitors in question, aluminum electrolytics used in radio power supplies, suffered from corrosive electrolyte leak-age—a major industry problem. Finally, the buyer turned and said, "Well, Mr. Sprague, you've been pretty quiet. What do you have to say?" R.C. leaned forward and picked up the Sprague unit, noting as he did so, "Ours don't leak!" The blotter was dry only where the Sprague unit had been sitting; a ring of electrolyte was gradually spreading from beneath all the competing units. In 1962, Sprague Electric adopted the slogan, "Second to None in Quality," followed by "Sprague—The Mark of Reliability." HYREL (short for High Reliability) became a Sprague trademark and, during World War II and the Korean and Cold Wars that followed, this reputation led military contractors to repeatedly turn to Sprague for the solution to unique electronic component problems.

Still, as the European storm clouds gathered, Sprague Specialties continued to struggle. Starting with a brief one-day strike in 1936, for the first time relations between labor and management became an issue. In the mid-1930s, the United Electrical, Radio, and Machine Workers of America (or UE), an affiliate of the CIO, began to organize production workers and machinists at equipment companies such as GE, Westinghouse, RCA, Philco, and others, until by 1943 their contracts covered nearly 600,000 workers in the electrical and radio industries[9].

During most of the 1930s there had been relatively little labor strife at Sprague Specialties. This was due in no small part to the

---

9   Raymond C. Bliss, *A Study of Union History at the Sprague Electric Compa-ny in North Adams, MA, 1929-1970* (unpublished thesis in partial fulfillment of requirements for BA in History from Williams College), pp. 9–14.

fact that the production workers in the company were represented by independent unions, initially Independent Condenser
Workers #1 (ICW # 1) and then ICW #2. The power of the
ICW lay in its six-man Grievance Board, which usually met with
management monthly to informally discuss and resolve grievances. Labor contracts were negotiated on an annual basis, allowing
for incremental changes in wages and benefits. The company also
worked hard to keep a family-like "we are all in this together"
relationship with its workforce. Working conditions were good,
management had an "open door" policy, and during lean times,

Aluminum capacitor assembly in Beaver Street Mill
Photo courtesy of North Adams Historical Society

when there were difficulties meeting payroll, the company offered inexpensive fifty- cent stocks to its employees. Although these had no real value at the time, for those employees who kept the stock there was a very hefty return years later, especially in the early to mid-1960s. Following a mid-January 1938 talk by Carl Shugg to the ICW #1 on the seriousness of the company's financial situation, the union compliantly agreed to take a temporary 10 percent wage reduction, which was rescinded as business improved.

Against this labor backdrop, there was progress on the R&D front: Reviewing a dismal 1938 in the January 1939 issue of *The Sprague Log* (a newsy internal company periodical), R.C. reported the introduction of two important new product families: a line of "atom" small etched dry electrolytic capacitors and, for the first time, a fixed resistor product line, a major diversification beyond capacitors. This really was the beginning of a new corporate strategy, which would be greatly accelerated by World War II, to become a full-service supplier of not only capacitors, but many different types of electronic components. A year later, R.C. reported a 1939 sales increase of 20 percent over 1938, production of a record fifty million units, employment at a record thirteen hundred people, and potential new markets in television and FM radio. The increasing importance of Sprague Specialties to the local community was also seen in 1939, when more than eighty different North Adams-based suppliers provided goods and services to the company.

While sales and profits dipped slightly in 1940, as it became evident that the US would eventually be drawn into what was still a European war, the switch to a wartime economy also began. In July 1940, Sprague Specialties and the Wall-Streeter Shoe Company jointly bid successfully against fifty-six other firms on a $172,000 trial government contract to manufacture gas masks for possible civilian deployment. A shoe company might seem like a strange partner, but when it was learned that stitching was a major part of the manufacturing process, R.C. turned to Wall-Streeter president and friend James E. Wall for help. The Brown Street plant was renovated and set up as a special facility to manufacture military products, including a test laboratory where products were stress tortured to determine life expectancy. Production of the gas masks began initially at the Brown Street plant in January 1941 by the Wall-Streeter fitting division under the supervision of Mitchell F. Nejame, moving in mid-1943 to leased space in the Arnold Print Works complex on Marshall Street. Multiple add-on orders continued until April 1944, when production was terminated.

JLS: *I remember trying on one of the masks. They were claustrophobic, had an awful smell, and luckily were never required. As Brown Street also began to manufacture incendiary bombs, I watched experiments of thermite material burning its way through quarter-inch or thicker steel plates.*

Towards the end of 1940, Carleton Shugg resigned as production manager to return to shipbuilding. While he would be missed, his excellent replacement was Amos Carey, who came from RCA with extensive experience in the manufacture of US government and military equipment. Carey's responsibilities quickly expanded, as first Brown Street and then Marshall Street cranked up to manufacture a wealth of increasingly complex electronic components and materials for wartime applications.

The October 27, 1940, issue of the *North Adams Transcript* reported that Sprague Specialties had submitted bids for components for a new type of incendiary bomb. There was little other information since "Army regulations forbid comment on the work." Less than a month later, the newspaper carried another article, saying it was rumored that the company had received an $800,000 order to make bomb parts. The company again refused comment, and after that there was mostly silence, except for an article on Defense Programs in the May 1941 issue of *The Sprague Log*. It reported production of various types of capacitors for Army and Navy communications gear and stated that Brown Street was being specifically tooled as a "defense plant." A year later, a June 1, 1942, telegram from Major General William N. Porter, Chief of the Chemical Warfare Service, would report that incendiary bombs manufactured in the Brown Street plant (actually Sprague made the bomb casings, which were filled with the explosive elsewhere) had been dropped over Tokyo and several other Japanese cities during Colonel James ("Jimmy") Doolittle's daring April 18, 1942, carrier raid off the USS Hornet. The company was rapidly transforming itself into much more than just a capacitor manufacturer and seemed ready to undertake just about anything.

In September 1941, there was a more serious nine-day wildcat strike, with workers demanding a 15 percent wage increase, although ICW #2 had already negotiated a 5 percent increase to run until March 1942. Behind many of these demands were efforts by the UE, which represented GE's large manufacturing complex in nearby Pittsfield, to gain representation rights for the Sprague workers. These efforts failed, and while the company did make concessions, the September 24, 1941, settlement largely favored management. But labor unrest did not cease, and the UE kept trying to make inroads as company financial performance continued to improve and employment approached three thousand, making Sprague Specialties an increasingly attractive plum to pick. The next serious challenge came right after V-J Day and led to an extremely contentious six-week strike.

While the gas mask and incendiary bomb orders in 1940 and 1941 had anticipated a much broader future involvement in what was still primarily a European conflict, the nation was not yet completely committed, and pockets of isolationism existed across the country. The United States' geographic separation from much of the world contributed to this; bombs were not falling on the US, and although American volunteers were dying in distant lands, it didn't seem that the country was directly threatened. In R.C. Sprague's Christmas message in the December 1941 Log (obviously written before December 7), he gave a very mixed message: "To preserve our country and to put down surely those who would replace our Bible with *Mein Kampf*, we must hold fast to our belief in the need for good will among men. Let us, therefore, celebrate this holiday season with good cheer and keep the hearts of our children bright with the Spirit of Christmas. And now looking forward to 1942, it is not going to be easy. It will be hard. So let us all together put our shoulders to the wheel in this common cause and PUSH – ON – TO – VICTORY in 1942, 1943, or however long it takes." Little did anyone know just how long and difficult World War II would be.

WORLD WAR II
—

At five to eight on the morning of Sunday, December 7, 1941, nearly two hundred Japanese torpedo bombers, dive bombers, and fighters, which had been launched undetected from the Japanese fleet some 275 miles north of Hawaii, swept unimpeded over Pearl Harbor on the Hawaiian island of Oahu, where the bulk of the United States' Pacific fleet lay sleeping and unprotected. In one devastating moment, "the date which will live in infamy" obliterated isolationism in the United States and unleashed the world's greatest economic engine. Sprague Specialties and thousands of other US firms were ready to make essential contributions to the victory that would take place four long years later.

Even as the United States implemented a full wartime economy, The Sprague Log continued its almost sunny outlook on the progress towards victory and peace. There was less news about sports and social events, less about what the company was actually doing to support the war effort, more letters of congratulations from customers on the delivery of war-related components, an increased emphasis on how to "do better" in wartime, and continual urging in issue after issue to purchase war bonds. But the Log had always been about people, marriages, and births, and now the tone gradually changed. From the beginning, women had made up the bulk of the manufacturing employees at Sprague Specialties and similar companies. This increased even more as husbands, sons, brothers, and lovers were sent to the Pacific, Atlantic, and Europe, some to return seriously injured and some never to return at all. There was more and more news from the front, more censored letters about how the writer's own personal war was going, and increasing reports of fateful "Gold Star" telegrams, letters, and personal visits.

Because there were no annual reports until 1945, and because much of the work was classified, piecing together the war years at Sprague Electric requires a variety of different sources, including the 1958 Newcomen report, internal company documents, a special July 12, 1960, issue of the North Adams Transcript, other Transcript articles published during World War II, a Williams

College thesis by Raymond Bliss[10], and issues of The Sprague Log during the war years. We know that it was a tumultuous period of extraordinary growth followed by temporary decline (see Table 1 in Appendix One) and that Sprague Electric emerged a much stronger company, well on its way to becoming a worldwide powerhouse in the electronic components industry.

Looking back, the accomplishments of Sprague Specialties/ Sprague Electric and the contributions that they made to the war effort between 1940 and 1945 were miraculous. In 1940, sales were slightly over $2 million, there were only some thirteen hundred employees in one plant (Beaver Street), and the primary product line was aluminum capacitors for commercial radio power supplies. When the war ended in 1945, sales had grown eightfold, employees were now located in three plants and numbered more than three thousand out of a North Adams population of roughly twenty-two thousand, and the company had made substantial contributions to the war effort, including microwave airborne search radar, the VT-Fuze, and atomic weaponry.

Employment continued to grow as more and more electronic components and other war-related products poured out of Beaver Street, Brown Street, rented space in the Arnold Print Works facility on Marshall Street, and six other subcontractors within 150 miles of North Adams, including the Rock of Ages Capacitor Corporation in Barre, Vermont, which specialized in manufacturing film capacitors and was eventually purchased by Sprague Electric. In April 1943 there was a major celebration in North Adams, to honor all the work that had been done so far.

---

10   Ibid.

As reported in a "Sprague Day" special edition of the *Transcript*, on April 2, 1943, Brig. Gen. A. A. Farmer and Captain J. S. Evans of the War and Navy Departments came to North Adams to present Sprague Specialties with the coveted Army-Navy "E" Award "for high achievement in war production." The ceremony was held at the Brown Street plant and attended by a host of dignitaries, including Massachusetts Governor Leverett Saltonstall. All Sprague employees were in attendance, and each was presented with an "E" pin and certificate. In an emotional acceptance speech, R.C. Sprague described how the 'E' Award was originally conceived by the US Navy in 1906, initially to recognize excellence in gunnery and later in engineering and communications. Since the start of the War, he explained, the significance of the 'E' had been broadened to include recognition for outstanding performance on the production front. Before the end of World War II, Sprague plants would receive four more such stars; the fact that less than 5 percent of all war plants received an "E" award during this period emphasizes just how distinguished such honors were and how well they served the reputation and subsequent growth of Sprague.

Gas masks and incendiary bombs were obviously significant war items, but *North Adams Transcript* articles hinted at even more noteworthy contributions[11]. As part of the super-secret Manhattan Project (the code name at Sprague was "Manhattan Square"), a team led by research director Dr. Preston Robinson designed, and Sprague produced, a special energy storage capacitor. These devices were used in the trigger mechanisms of the first atomic bomb exploded at Alamogordo, New Mexico, and the nuclear weapons that were subsequently dropped over Hiroshima and

---

11 *North Adams Transcript*, September 22, 1943.

Nagasaki, Japan, bringing World War II to an abrupt and horrifying end. After the war, Sprague Electric continued to supply the capacitors for the United States' growing production of atomic and nuclear weapons.

One of the most important of Sprague's wartime contributions was the design of special capacitors for the US Navy's VT proximity fuze, with Dr. Robinson again heading the design team. Located in the nose of a projectile, the fuze was a rugged and complex miniature five-vacuum-tube radio and receiving device, which caused the shell to explode if it passed within a predetermined distance, say seventy feet, of the target, rather than on contact or by a preset timing device. Production began in September 1942, and the first successful hit was made on January 5, 1943, when the cruiser USS Helena shot down a Japanese plane using a VT-fuzed shell. The device played a dominant role in combating Japanese kamikaze attacks late in the war, while the Army version, which had been held in reserve until the critical Battle of the Bulge, was credited in helping blunt the German offensive and saving thousands of American lives. At its peak, Sprague employed twenty-four hundred on the project. (On October 1, 1945, R.C. Sprague announced that, in addition to the five Army-Navy "E" Awards, the company had been awarded the Navy Bureau of Ordinance "E" Award for its role in the development and manufacture of the VT fuze, one of only thirty-six firms so honored out of the thousand that participated in the program[12].)

Meanwhile, other changes were under way. On April 24, 1944, the company officially changed its name from Sprague Specialties

---

12 *North Adams Transcript*, September 24, 1945 and October 1, 1945.

to Sprague Electric Company, a name felt to be more representa-tive of its businesses and also reflective of the company that Frank. J. Sprague had sold to GE in 1902. To allow room for further expansion, in August 1944 Sprague purchased the former Arnold Print Works complex at 87 Marshall Street in North Ad-ams from the Beacon Realty and Trading Company, which had acquired the property in 1942 when Arnold Print Works went bankrupt and ceased operations[13]. The complex had grown to cover thirteen acres, with twenty-six stone- and brick-built build-ings connected by dozens of interconnecting bridges and tunnels. The site was a village unto itself, with vast courtyards formed by the spaces between the buildings and over four thousand win-dows—the legacy of textile manufacturing in the nineteenth century—glittering across the façade.

As the wars in Europe and the Pacific moved inexorably to their conclusions, detailed planning for the transition, or "reconver-sion" as it was called, began at Sprague Electric and throughout the country. Prices had been fixed by law since 1941, and postwar increases would have to be negotiated. Almost everything Sprague made was related to the war effort, and major cancellations were expected. Although fighting on both fronts continued unabated, friction on the labor front began to intensify. As negotiations for the fall 1944 labor contracts started, Local #249 of the CIO's United Electrical Radio and Machine Workers of America (UE), led by Gerry Steinberg, announced it would once more seek representation of Sprague's workforce. But a new and powerful influence had joined Sprague's ICW #2. William Stackpole, who came from GE Pittsfield and was violently opposed to the UE, moved to Sprague Electric in the middle of the fray (two months

---

13   *North Adams Transcript*, November 25, 1944.

later he became chairman of the powerful ICW #2 Grievance Committee, a position he would hold for more than twenty years). He attacked the UE as being both useless and communist leaning (a common tactic nationwide at the time), and when the election was held in late August, the UE was again defeated[14].

With the German forces vanquished and Hitler dead, Victory in Europe Day took place on May 8, 1945. Still, the Japanese fought on until the first atomic bombs were dropped on Hiroshima and Nagasaki, and World War II officially ended on Victory in Japan Day, August 22, 1945. Reconversion began across the United States and at Sprague Electric, where 80 percent or some $8.5 million of the outstanding orders were indeed cancelled. Sprague immediately terminated its six subcontractors and moved to lay off workers and temporarily close Marshall Street, concentrating operations on the Beaver and Brown Street plants with a reduced workweek. Prior to V-J Day, total Sprague employment in North Adams was twenty-six hundred, a number that briefly dropped by more than one thousand people in less than a month. It quickly recovered as new orders came in, but not until after significant damage had been done on the labor front.

The May 4, 1945, issue of the *North Adams Transcript* had reported that "1,523 at Sprague's in Favor of Strike" if a satisfactory new contract wasn't reached. In October there was a two-day walkout in response to the company's reconversion plans, and then an emboldened ICW #2, led by William Stackpole, demanded an across-the-board 30 percent (later reduced to 22 percent) wage increase to make up for lost income caused by the shortened workweeks. A bitter six-week strike was finally settled

---

14   *North Adams Transcript*, August 31, 1944.

on December 16, 1945, with terms that clearly favored the company. In addition, since the transition from military to civilian orders was only in its early stages, while the workers forfeited income during the six weeks, the lost production made little impact on the customers. A terse comment from R.C. summarized the result: "Like most employers in the country [following the end of the war], we found ourselves faced with labor unrest. We were unable to come to an agreement on a wage increase, and a strike was called on November 1. After prolonged negotiations, an agreement was reached and the employees returned to work on December 17."

There were some later periods of unrest—and the UE, as well as several other national unions, continued their unrelenting representation assault—but with the exception of a five and a half month strike by some thirty machinists (who had affiliated with the International Association of Machinists in February 1949) in the latter half of 1949, there would not be another strike of production, office, and maintenance workers at Sprague until 1970. Several historians, including Raymond Bliss, have concluded that this was due to the weakness of both the UE and ICW #2[15]. There is, however, another possible conclusion: during the extended period of growth and prosperity at Sprague following the end of World War II, ICW #2 was able to fairly represent the workers' needs and demands—and Sprague Electric was an exemplary place to work.

After being in business since 1926, Sprague Electric issued its first annual report to stockholders for the year ended December 31, 1945. Despite reconversion difficulties, net sales totaled

15   Bliss, *A Study of Union History*, p. 33.

$16,724,298, profit after tax $653,913, and cash on hand $2,113,270, a very good start for the next growth period. The annual report included several other notable comments: of the 551 Sprague employees who had served in the armed services, a sobering eighteen "made the supreme sacrifice." More than 90 percent of those discharged from the military had already returned to work at Sprague. Pent-up demand for radios, household appliances, automobiles, and other consumer products was expected to fuel the need for electronic components such as capacitors, and it was expected that equipment manufacturers would buy from "long-established suppliers [such as Sprague] who are known for high-quality and on-time delivery."

Not anticipated in this forecast were renewed military requirements that soon resulted from the Korean War, the increasing tensions between the United States and the USSR as the Cold War heated up, and the introduction of television. Sprague Electric was poised to begin a long and productive growth period.

CHAPTER FIVE

SPRAGUE ELECTRIC COMPANY (1946–1975)

COLD WAR, SPACE, TELEVISION, COMPUTERS, SEMICONDUCTORS

—

Sprague Electric's wartime sales peaked in 1944 at $20.8 million and then dropped steadily over the next three years as the US transitioned from a wartime to peacetime economy. Revenues in 1947 reached a low point of $10.5 million, although the company was still able to eke out a small profit. Employment had also dropped to only twenty-one hundred. But the decline was short lived, as demand for new consumer products such as televisions surged, and the illusion of World War II as "the war to end all wars" was shattered when the North Koreans, backed by China and Russia, swarmed across the 38th Parallel on June 25, 1950, and the Cold War began in earnest. By 1953 revenues had grown to $46.8 million, profits to $2.89 million, and employment reached an all-time high of fifty-five hundred worldwide. More detailed financial results between 1945 and 1953 can be found in Table 1 in Appendix One.

GROWTH AND EXPANSION

—

In order to meet increased demand in both the consumer and military markets, Sprague Electric launched a branch plant program in the neighboring states of Vermont (Barre), New Hampshire (Concord and Nashua), and, over the next ten years, California (Visalia), Puerto Rico (Ponce), and Italy (Milan). R.C. also began to branch out when in 1945 he became a director of the Associated Industries of Massachusetts (he was elected president in 1951), the first step in an ever-increasing involvement at both the state and federal levels. Years later, in discussing this expansion of his personal horizon with his grandson, David, he commented, "It is my nature that when I join something I either participate, I hope constructively, or get out."[1] Following the end of World War II he would have ample opportunity to demonstrate this important aspect of his personality. But R.C. was only part of the Sprague story.

By the late 1920s, all three of electrical inventor Frank J. Sprague's sons—R.C., Julian K., and Frank D. (plant engineer/ mechanical engineer)—worked for Sprague Specialties Company. In addition to these three brothers, R.C.'s two sons—Bob Jr. and John—played major roles in the history of Sprague Electric Company. Each Sprague possessed different skills and influenced the direction of the company in different ways as it grew and matured. R.C. was a unique combination of an engineer and a businessman, but he had ambitions well beyond his company and even the electronics industry. Julian was the consummate salesman but also saw himself as much more. When Bob Jr. joined the company right after World War II, he was only twenty-three and

---

1   Robert C. Sprague, interviewed by his grandson, David Sprague, 1985.

had attended only one year of college. He had innate mechanical skills—in later life he collected and restored Stanley Steamer antique cars—and excelled at flying airplanes. He rose through the human resources discipline to become a senior vice president, but his greatest love was to be in the air, a passion that eventually led to his death.

JULIAN KING SPRAGUE

—

Julian King Sprague was born in New York City on June 14, 1903, the second son of Frank J. Sprague and his second wife, Harriet Chapman Jones. He attended Hotchkiss and then Yale, which he never finished, and after several different jobs joined Sprague Specialties in 1926 as production manager. Several field sales jobs followed, and he rose rapidly within the sales organization leading to his 1945 election as vice president for sales. One of his most outstanding innovations was the creation of the applications or field engineering department to complement the central sales organization. He became deeply involved in many industry and government activities and in 1954 was appointed chairman of the Advisory Board on Electronic Parts for the Department of Defense.

When his brother, R.C., went to Washington in 1953, Julian was elected president of Sprague Electric, a position he held until his death in 1960. Even as illness began to overwhelm him in the late 1950s, he continued his frantic work schedule, including a 1959 visit to the USSR to evaluate Soviet manufacturing techniques. A lifelong smoker, he was diagnosed with lung cancer in April 1960, but a month later still chaired a nine-person team charged by the Department of Defense with seeking cooperative ways of sharing research in electronic parts and materials with France and

England.

In July 1960, Julian entered Massachusetts General Hospital to undergo radical surgery and radiation treatment, but to no avail. He died on September 27 at his Big Bend Ranch in Texas.

ROBERT CHAPMAN SPRAGUE JR.

—

Robert Chapman Sprague Jr. (Bob Jr.) was born in Brookline, Massachusetts, on December 30, 1922. He attended Middlesex School and studied for one year at Williams College before Pearl Harbor ended his college education. Already an experienced pilot, during most of World War II he served as an FAA Flight Instructor for the Army Air Corps. In 1946 he joined Sprague Electric in human resources, and in 1951 started Sprague Flight Operations, a small but active corporate department used primarily to ferry management, sales, technical, and support personnel to branch plants along the East Coast.

In 1953, Bob joined the Sprague board of directors, and in 1958 completed his renewed formal education when he graduated from MIT as a Sloan Fellow. Promoted to senior vice president in 1960, he took on added responsibilities in purchasing and facilities management and in 1964 became senior vice president of corporate services, a position he held until his retirement in 1980. Besides his corporate responsibilities, he was active in both electronics industry and local civic affairs and was a colonel in the Civil Air Patrol and Commander of the Northern Berkshire Squadron. Continuing his passion for flying after retirement, in the mid-1980s Bob built a high- performance Christen Eagle biplane from a kit, the plane he was flying when he was killed in a horrifying crash on April 10, 1987, at the North Adams Harriman-West Airport. It was the blackest of days for the Sprague family.

Another key executive, Ernest L. Ward, joined the company in early 1946 as a vice president, an unusual addition since Ernie's background was in investment banking, while his Sprague responsibilities began in manufacturing[2]. (Previously, he had worked in Chicago as a partner of the investment banking firm, F. S. Moseley.) As manufacturing was being diversified to increasing numbers of branch plants throughout the United States and the world, what the company needed was a brilliant executive who could attract and motivate good people and effectively evaluate and improve their performance. Ernie moved up the management ladder rapidly, first to executive vice president in 1952 and then president in 1960, after Julian's death.

As 1946 ended, the company had nearly completed its peacetime conversion and once more was pursuing consumer markets such as AM and FM radios, automotive radios, phonograph console systems, and television—the next great market opportunity. As glimmers of the upcoming Cold War intensified, Sprague Electric employed specific basic strategies during the growth period that followed, pursuing both civilian and military markets, offering superior performance and reliability compared to the competition, continuing component miniaturization, broadening the product portfolio, and seeking geographic plant diversification worldwide. Ten years after the end of World War II, the four manufacturing locations had grown to thirteen worldwide, employment had more than doubled, and Sprague Electric was flourishing.

---

2   *The Sprague Log*, March 9, 1946.

New products fueled growth, many of which had been developed internally during the war: "coupling" capacitors to enable telephone service in rural areas over electric power lines, pulse-forming networks for radar equipment, noise-suppression filters for both civilian and military equipment, miniature molded tubular paper capacitors, and a miniature metal-clad hermetically sealed capacitor line for military equipment such as proximity fuzes and guided missiles. In addition, the Nashua, New Hampshire, plant was awarded a large government contract for VT fuze printed circuit amplifiers (complex assemblies of resistors and capacitors deposited on ceramic substrates). Later this technology developed into a major business in coupling and decoupling networks for the computer industry, especially IBM.

Growth also resulted from acquisitions, such as the 1948 purchase of Milwaukee-based Herlec Corporation, which provided Sprague Electric the technology for disc ceramic, multi-layer vitreous enamel structures and printed circuit applications. These technologies led to Sprague's development of the multi-layer ceramic capacitor (MLCC), a product family that today dominates the entire capacitor industry, although Sprague Electric was never able to capitalize on its first-to-market position.

Discrete capacitors always constituted the core of Sprague Electric's business, and it became a worldwide leader. However, as the company expanded its product base into other types of electronic devices and materials, there was one more ingredient about to enter the mix and revolutionize not just the electronics industry, but the entire world.

Sampling of Sprague Electric's more than 10,000 different passive components, c. 1950. Photo courtesy of author

THE TRANSISTOR

—

So far only passive electronic components (such as capacitors, resistors, and inductors) have been discussed; these devices, while vital in any electronic circuit, cannot provide amplification or gain to an electrical signal. Until the late 1940s, amplification could be accomplished only by using vacuum tubes. Even in miniature form these active devices were large, consumed a great deal of electrical power, and, as circuitry became increasingly complex (such as in the early digital computers ENIAC and EDIAC that were developed toward the end of World War II), were notoriously unreliable. The Holy Grail in electronics was the solid state amplifier, which had been pursued worldwide since the 1920s.

Just prior to the war, one of the greatest collections of technical talent concentrated on attaining this goal was at the Bell Telephone Laboratory (Bell Labs or BTL), at the time the research and development arm of AT&T in Murray Hill, New Jersey.

During the war, this work at BTL was temporarily discontinued in order to concentrate on the wartime communications business of AT&T. However, wartime experience clearly demonstrated the need for such a device, and extensive government-sponsored research and development on germanium (Ge) and silicon (Si), the principal materials then used in microwave radar detectors, laid the basis for the first operational solid state amplifiers. In late 1945, Mervin J. Kelley at BTL created the Solid State Research Laboratory, loaded with talent and with the mission to develop a practical solid-state amplifier using either Ge or Si. Only a little over two years later, on December 23, 1947, John Bardeen and Walter H. Brattain officially demonstrated such a device, a crude Ge point contact transistor. This device was, and still is, difficult to understand and even harder to make, and one month later their brilliant associate, William B. Shockley, conceived the more practical "junction transistor," whose first operational realization appeared in early 1950. For their discoveries, the three men shared the 1956 Nobel Prize for Physics[3].

At first these results caused only a modest stir, but, as their true importance began to sink in, corporations from around the world clamored to jump on the bandwagon and gain associated licenses and know-how agreements with Western Electric, the production arm of AT&T and licenser of the patents. By the time of the

---

3   For more on the history of the transistor, see Sprague, Revitalizing US
    Electronics, pp. 18–19; and Bo Lojek, History of Semiconductor Engineering
    (Berlin/Heidelberg: Springer-Verlag, 2007).

third Western Electric "Transistor Symposium" in April 1952, there were twenty-six domestic and fourteen foreign attendees. Included in the list of licensees was Sprague Electric. For Sprague this was a cataclysmic decision and, at least in the minds of some, a fatal mistake.

While the company was trying to figure out how to enter the business, it launched an internal research and development effort in North Adams that included hiring a number of foreign-born engineers who were being brought into this country by the US Signal Corps. The most important and talented of these was Czech-born Dr. Kurt Lehovec, who was hired by Preston Robinson in mid-1952 to head up the Sprague Electric semiconductor research effort. Since Bardeen, Brattain, and Shockley had announced their discoveries, a number of different approaches for making Ge or Si transistors had been developed. Because of production difficulties with the original point contact device, the preferred device structure quickly became the junction transistor, in which the required dopants were introduced into a single crystal germanium (or silicon) die or wafer by alloying, high-temperature diffusion, or a combination of both. Lehovec first developed an improved point contact transistor and then started to work on junction devices, including the creation of multiple p-n junctions in crystalline Ge. This led to US Patent #3,029,366, Multiple Semiconductor Assembly (filed on April 22, 1959, and issued on April 10, 1962), Sprague's first integrated circuit patent.

JOHN L. SPRAGUE RECALLS: *In September 1958, Jack Kilby of Texas Instruments (TI) demonstrated the first semiconductor integrated circuit (IC), and after the related patent was issued in June 1964 TI began patent interference proceedings against IC manufacturers around the world, including Sprague Electric. Although Kilby's ugly little circuit was* *completely useless as a producible device, it proved the concept, and therefore the potential financial implications from licensing were huge. Panic ensued throughout the industry, especially among the smaller manufacturers such as Sprague Electric, which had very limited semiconductor patent portfolios of its own to cross- license. At first, even Kurt Lehovec's patent didn't seem to carry much weight since it described a device structure that was never going to be industry practice. At Kurt's request, I studied the patent in detail, becoming increasingly excited. As far as I could tell, almost hidden in the description, claims, and illustrations, Kurt had patented the basic technique used throughout the industry for electrically isolating the different elements within an integrated circuit. Initially, Kurt disagreed, but we soon reached consensus, and Kurt and the Sprague patent attorney were well armed for the interference hearing with Texas Instruments. It was like David and Goliath—semiconductor giant TI couldn't believe the final decision.*

In March 1966, the US Patent Office ruled that Lehovec had the basic patent covering p-n junction isolation in ICs, by far Sprague Electric's most momentous semiconductor patent. Kilby was awarded the 2000 Nobel Prize in Physics for his 1958 invention, but Lehovec's work earned him recognition as a co-inventor of the integrated circuit[4].

On the other hand Philco Corporation, up to this time known primarily as a radio manufacturer, took a completely new direction, and in 1954 invented the surface barrier transistor (SBT) in which electrochemical etching accurately defined an extreme-

---

4   Lojek, p. 2.

ly thin base region, and doping metals were electrochemically deposited on this base. Along with improved next-generation devices such as the MAT (micro alloy type) and MADT (micro alloyed diffused base), the Philco transistors were the world's fastest switching transistors for the remainder of the 1950s, and were used in what was the first commercially available solid state computer, the Philco S-2000 Transac introduced in 1957. It was the Philco approach that Sprague initially decided to follow in its transistor venture.

It is unclear how Sprague Electric made this decision, since it appears that Lehovec had little, if any, input. Perhaps it was the speed advantage, although this would disappear in late 1959 with the Bell Labs invention of the epitaxial transistor[5]. For many years Philco had been Sprague's largest customer, and there were excellent relations at the management level, so perhaps R.C. Sprague didn't want to be just another Bell licensee, or was enamored with the superb Philco high-speed mechanization (which the process required because each semiconductor die had to be individually handled). The competing MESA transistor process, which evolved from the basic junction transistor with all its initial limitations, was nonetheless a more efficient batch process. Moreover, by 1960 oxide masking and junction protection, combined with epitaxy in a planar construction with a flat surface, would not only eliminate the limitations in the junction transistor process, but also allow deposited surface interconnections to form integrated circuits.

---

5   In epitaxy, a thin lightly doped single crystal layer of, for example, Si can be grown on the surface of a heavily doped Si substrate. This causes reduction in the resistance of the collector region of a MESA transistor, thus eliminating the performance advantage held by the electrochemical transistor.

Nonetheless, Sprague continued to pour money into the electro-chemical approach in its Concord, New Hampshire, plant, and by the mid-1960s had a modest annualized $10 million semicon-ductor business with a forecast of doubling over the next year or two. However, led by Fairchild Semiconductor Corporation (a subsidiary of Fairchild Camera and Instrument), planar technol-ogy came to dominate the semiconductor industry, and by 1973 electrochemical transistors had become only a small specialty business at Sprague. By then, Sprague Electric had jumped full force into planar technology. Appendix Two gives a more detailed timeline of the development of the planar process which, with many variations, is the dominant technology still used today in the more than $300 billion worldwide integrated circuit market.

While the transistor was creating both technological turmoil and opportunity in the electronics industry, and the Korean and Cold Wars were creating explosive growth for companies such as Sprague Electric, a series of events was about to have a major impact on the company at the management level.

R.C. GOES TO WASHINGTON

—

"On January 12, 1953, Robert C. Sprague resigned as President [Julian K. Sprague was elected to replace him as president and Bob Sprague Jr. to replace him as a director] to accept assignment as Undersecretary of the Air Force, which after four weeks did not materialize because of his unwillingness to sell his substantial stock interest in the Sprague Electric Company which, although not required by law, the [Eisenhower] administration felt neces-sary in view of the action by the Senate Armed Services Commit-tee on the appointments of Charles E. Wilson, Robert Keyes, and two Service Secretaries who also had substantial stock interests. On March 24, 1953, Mr. Sprague rejoined the company as Chairman of the Board of Directors."[6]

In David Sprague's 1985 interview, his grandfather provided additional colorful insight into this aborted appointment. "Your grandmother was violently opposed, arguing that she didn't like Washington and wanted nothing to do with politics which, in her opinion, was a 'dirty business.' She even went so far as to say that if I decided to go to Washington, it would be without her. Not really believing she would carry out this threat, I accepted the nomination, subject to the results of scheduled follow-up meetings with Secretary of the Air Force nominee Harold Talbott (who would be my boss) and President-elect Eisenhower. One of the key questions was whether or not I would have to sell my Sprague Electric stock in order to eliminate any conflict of interest, as had other nominees such as Talbott himself (a director of Chrysler) and Secretary of Defense Charles Wilson (former General Motors president). Since I had resigned all my Sprague Electric positions and Sprague Electric did not supply assembled end equipment either for civilian or military use, I didn't see a problem, and Eisenhower agreed. However, the Senate Armed Services Committee had other ideas and when I was asked directly by Talbott and Wilson if I would agree to sell my stock, and I declined, the nomination was withdrawn, and in early February 1953 I returned to the Berkshires, at least for the moment."

JLS: *By coincidence, I was in Washington during part of the time my father was going through the confirmation process. As First Lieutenant and Gunnery Officer on the USS Klein-*

---

6   Sprague Electric Annual Report, 1952.

smith (APD 134), I was attending the Navy's 20 and 40 mm Gunnery School in DC. I could tell that my father was bitten by the Washington bug: he was both certain he could make a real contribution and it would be an entirely new adventure. So he was deeply disappointed when his nomination fell apart, although this was short lived as only seven months later he became even more deeply involved in the issues of continental defense and nuclear deterrence between the United States and Russia. When asked why he refused to sell his Sprague Electric shares, he said this might have allowed control of the company to pass to some outside entity and thus adversely affect the North Adams economy and the thousands of its citizens employed by Sprague Electric. He was unwilling to let this happen.

Today it is easy to forget how dangerous a period it was at the beginning of the Cold War, especially after the USSR exploded its first nuclear bomb in 1949. Things only intensified when Sputnik, the first man-made satellite, was sent into orbit by the Soviets in October 1957. There was very real concern about all-out nuclear war between the United States and Russia. People who could afford it were beginning to build bomb shelters in their homes. New museums such as the Sterling and Francine Clark Art Institute were located in places such as Williamstown, Massachusetts, rather than New York City, in order to hopefully escape any potential nuclear blast zone. And a new term, "mega deaths" (millions of casualties), began to appear in secret government-sponsored reports that analyzed the results of different war-gaming scenarios.

In September 1953, R.C. was approached by former Massachu-setts Governor Leverett Saltonstall (who was now a US senator and chairman of the Preparedness Subcommittee of the Senate

Armed Services Committee) to chair a committee tasked with making an in-depth study and report on the Russian nuclear first-strike capability against the US using intercontinental bombers. As it turned out, because of the sensitivity of the information he would be receiving he ended up being the only member of this "committee," although he did have staff support and full-time use of former President Roosevelt's "Air Force One" DC-4. He never resigned as CEO of Sprague Electric, although the next four years of his life were consumed by this assignment. As recounted in David's interview, R.C.'s narrative of these years makes fascinating reading, and excerpts can be found in Appendix Three.

With the submission of his report and the almost simultaneous appointment of James Killian as Eisenhower's science advisor, R.C. Sprague's formal involvement in continental defense was over, except for his position as a trustee of MITRE (a nonprofit that manages federally funded R&D centers), and he returned to Sprague Electric as full-time chairman of the board, treasurer, and chief executive officer. After five years spent obsessing about saving the United States and the rest of the free world from nuclear annihilation, one can only speculate how he personally felt about returning to "normalcy."

Not unexpectedly, Julian had been extremely excited about the opportunity to finally run the company as president, with his older brother in Washington as an Eisenhower appointee. He was disappointed when, only a few months later, R.C. was back as chairman and still in charge. There were inside reports of violent arguments between the two men and at least one public record that Julian opposed involvement in semiconductors, while R.C. saw this as the next great leap forward for Sprague Electric. So how did the company perform during this period? In fact, sales were flat in the $42 to $46 million range, although profits gradually decreased during the period (see Table 1 in Appendix One).

THE DOLDRUMS: 1952 TO 1958
—

Despite flat revenues, 1952 to 1958 was a volatile period of transition before the next great growth spurt. The Korean War ended in July 1953, but the costly and dangerous Cold War and arms race with the USSR continued, as both nations enlarged their nuclear arsenals and missile and underwater capabilities, headed into space, and expanded their conventional weaponry. Despite the gradual decrease in Sprague's military sales from 1952 to 1958, this decline was almost exactly compensated by the expansion in television. At the same time, the 1947 invention of the transistor, followed only ten years later by the integrated circuit, dictated that the design and component requirements for electronic systems had to radically change as well. This seemed a perfect environment for Sprague Electric, with its reputation for superior performance and high reliability.

More worrisome was the continuing decrease in profits between 1953 and 1958, driven by the addition of facilities around the world in anticipation of the next growth period and skyrocketing overhead costs, especially in semiconductor research, development, and engineering (RD&E). In 1952, RD&E expenses totaled approximately $1 million or about 2.5 percent of sales. By 1966, they were just under $10 million and more than 6.5 percent. This point is critical. In the passive component industry, such expenses tend to run around 3 percent of sales, while in integrated circuits the number is double or triple this number, or even higher. Sprague Electric had to have a major success in semiconductors in order to afford the overhead structure it was creating. Otherwise the result would be a bloodbath, which is what eventually happened.

Sprague Electric's most important new product of the 1950s was the 150D solid tantalum capacitor. While the 150D was a hermetically sealed axial device, no matter how the solid tantalum body was configured or encapsulated, its small size, high volumetric efficiency, shock resistance, temperature stability, and use of a solid rather than liquid electrolyte made it truly revolutionary. It quickly found use across the whole spectrum of transistorized circuitry, with the importance of the market for industrial and military computers resulting in IBM eventually becoming Sprague Electric's largest customer.

Bell Labs is often credited with inventing this device, yet work on it actually began at Sprague in the early 1950s, led by Preston Robinson. His US Patent #3,066,247, "Electrolytic Device" (filed on August 25, 1954, and finally issued on November 27, 1962, after bitter litigation with Western Electric) was recognized as the controlling solid tantalum patent. The extreme miniaturization of the device resulted from the high surface area of the sintered tantalum anode and the high dielectric constant (25 versus 9 for alumina) of the tantalum pentoxide (Ta_2O_5) dielectric formed on the pellet. The solid MnO_2 electrolyte, which is created by thermal decomposition of manganese nitrate ($Mn<NO_3>_2$), accounts for the capacitor's extreme stability. From conception, Sprague Electric enjoyed, or shared with Kemet, the number-one position in worldwide market share, a market that was still $1 billion in 1987[7], even with the emergence of the "multilayer ceramic capacitor" (MLCC) as the dominant capacitor family at $3 billion. The

---

7   The year 1987 is cited since this was when Sprague began to disappear as an entity. This is covered in detail in Chapter Six.

worldwide aluminum capacitor market in 1987 was $2 billion[8].

Multilayer constructions (to increase the area and therefore the capacitance) were first introduced in the 1930s, using stacked layers of natural mica. Because these mica-based constructions had a low dielectric constant and relatively thick layers, and required an expensive process, mica was eventually replaced by synthetic dielectrics such as vitreous enamel, then titania (TiO_2), and finally barium titanate ($BaTiO_3$) formulations, whose dielectric constants can reach the thousands. As with solid tantalums, Sprague Electric was also an early leader. In 1958, based on work by Jack Fabricius and George Olsen using modified DuPont equipment originally designed to spray vitreous enamel layers, Sprague Electric introduced the first production multi-layer ceramic capacitor, named the Type 31 C MONOLYTHIC® capacitor. Its solid construction and high-volumetric efficiency made it especially useful for semiconductor circuitry. Its big advantages over solid tantalums are much cheaper materials, even greater volumetric efficiency, and the ability to use a very high degree of mechanization in manufacturing. Although there are applications for all the different dielectric systems, today the MLCC absolutely dominates the capacitor market, led by Japanese firms and their subsidiaries. Unfortunately, Sprague Electric never succeeded in being a factor in this segment of the capacitor industry.

BREAKOUT: 1959 TO 1966

—

As Sprague Electric became an increasingly important player on the world stage, R.C. began to expand the board of directors in

---

8   Sprague, *Revitalizing US Electronics*, p. 160.

1959 by adding outside members with both broad experience and name recognition. The first was Frederick R. Lack, an industry veteran who had recently retired after forty-seven years in the Bell System. Until his retirement from the board in 1974, he was a close confidant to R.C. and an early mentor and friend of John Sprague when he joined the company. More additions soon followed.

A more formalized system of long-range planning was created in 1959 with the establishment of the Fourth Decade Committee. Its mission was to plot a course for Sprague to profitably reach a minimum sales level of $100 million by 1967, which would parallel the Electronics Industry Association (EIA) growth estimate of 8 percent for the industry. R.C. Sprague was the committee's driving force, and he was joined by Julian Sprague, Ernie Ward, Neal Welch, Bill Nolan, Bill Lazier, Bob Sprague Jr., and Preston Robinson. It is interesting to note that, at least initially, there was no one on the committee who knew anything about semiconductor technology.

Nonetheless, Sprague Electric was already involved in semiconductors, spearheaded by Kurt Lehovec and later joined by John Sprague. Considering the importance of the integrated circuit in today's world, it is amazing to recognize the role Sprague engineers played in its early development, especially Lehovec's patent on PN Junction Isolation. Despite this pioneering effort, though, it would take Sprague Electric over thirteen years of struggle to finally create a viable integrated circuit strategy and business.

In 1959, Sprague Electric revenues surged with the end of the 1958 US economic recession, strong growth in entertainment electronics (especially television), robust military purchases, and new products such as the solid tantalum capacitor. By 1966, the single most successful year in the company's history, revenues, profits, and employment reached $141.5 million, $8.7 million, and 12,500 respectively. (For more detail, see Table 2 in Appendix One.) The period from 1959 to 1966 was very strong for the entire domestic electronics industry, which reached nearly $20 billion in revenues by 1966, driven by industrial computers, data-processing, color TV, and the Vietnam War. While Sprague Electric was still feeling its way in semiconductors, it continued to gain market share in all the capacitor families, with the exception of the still-infant multi-layer ceramics market.

With the deaths of Julian Sprague and directors Frank Bond and Harry Robbins in 1960, more outsiders joined the board of directors, including Joseph A. Erickson (former president of the Federal Reserve Bank of Boston) and two prestigious MIT professors, Dr. Jerrold R. Zacharias and Dr. Jerome B. Weisner. Weisner resigned in January 1961, when he was appointed Science Advisor to President John F. Kennedy, but rejoined the board in 1964.

Sprague Electric's product portfolio continued to broaden, but it became clear that centralized control would no longer work, and the company began to create a series of operating divisions, each with its own manufacturing, engineering, and product marketing. The first of these was the Special Products Division (magnetic components and discrete component assemblies) in 1958, followed by the Transistor Division in 1960. Toward the end of 1960 the Resistor Division was created, and in 1963 Fred Scarborough formed the Filter Division. Still, overall management of the capacitor operations remained centralized for many more years, and these new "divisions" were not true profit-and-loss centers. All products were still sold through the powerful national sales organization (under vice president Carroll Killen), and pricing control was still centralized under Neal Welch, senior vice president for marketing and sales, and his inside sales group. However, this structure began to change in 1964, when the newly formed Semiconductor Division took control of its own pricing.

As the semiconductor effort began to absorb more and more of the company's resources, cultural differences became more evident between "old Sprague" (primarily passive components, with centralized control by older experienced managers, industry leadership and image, and the internal cash generator) and "new Sprague" (primarily semiconductors, with decentralized profit centers, much younger and often less-experienced managers, initially little industry image, and a consumer of the cash generated by the passives). This problem of two de facto Sprague Electrics was never completely resolved during the remaining life of the company. This was the situation that the author, John Louis Sprague, R.C. Sprague's younger son, stepped into in 1959 after receiving his PhD from Stanford University.

JOHN L. SPRAGUE

—

JLS: *I was born in Quincy, Massachusetts, on April 5, 1930, but grew up in Williamstown where I attended local schools before going away to Middlesex School in Concord, Massachusetts. I entered Princeton University in 1948 and graduated in 1952 with an AB in Chemistry as well as a Naval Reserve Officers Training Corps commission in the US Navy.*

My first employment at the company was during the summer of 1949 when I was a technician for (I believe) a Dr. Taylor, making electrical measurements on different types of capacitor dielectrics. He was a wonderful man who had been tortured as a Japanese POW during World War II, and as a result had to drink beakers of dilute hydrochloric acid before eating to replace the stomach acid his body no longer generated. During the two-plus months I was at 87 Marshall Street that summer, I probably spent more time in downtown North Adams than at any other time of my life. At noon I joined the thousand or so employees who poured out of the main gate and headed downtown for lunch, to shop, or just plain relax. My co-workers were all friendly, although as the boss's son I was treated as somewhat of a curiosity. Main Street was a wide, dynamic corridor, filled with shops of all description, diners and restaurants, bars, several hotels and a movie theatre. The east end was dominated by church spires, and there seemed to be people everywhere, talking, laughing, and enjoying life. In 1949, North Adams was a wonderfully upbeat place to wander around and explore.

With the Korean War still in full swing, I spent the three years after graduation on active duty; my first ship was the Kleinsmith. In the fall of 1953 I enrolled in the US Navy's Officers Electronics Material School at Treasure Island in the San Francisco Bay. As one of only two non-electrical engineers in a class of fifty, it was a tough haul, although during the six month crash course I received my first basic electrical engineering training, as well as an early introduction to semiconductor materials and devices.

My last duty posting was aboard the Navy's first (and last) command cruiser, the USS Northampton (ECLC-1/CLC-1), as Assistant Electronics Officer and Electronics Division Officer. Loaded with electronics, the Northampton served as a flagship for the Sixth Fleet in the Mediterranean from the fall of 1954 until the spring of 1955.

While at Treasure Island my wife, Jid, and I fell in love with northern California. So in the fall of 1955 I entered Stanford University as a PhD candidate in Physical Chemistry. By pure chance there was a professor, Claudio Alvarez-Tostado ("Butch"), who was studying silicon chemistry. So I happily settled into an unused dark room in the basement of one of the chemistry buildings, and started making crude germanium and silicon diodes and transistors, with Butch as my thesis advisor. During my research, I also received advice and some basic electronic equipment from Sprague Electric, where researcher—and former Luftwaffe pilot—Rainer Zuleeg was particularly helpful. Like all veterans, I was in a hurry and had completed all my requirements by the spring of 1959. My doctoral thesis, Studies on the Nature of Metal to Semiconductor Alloy Junctions, was particularly timely since the transistor had only been invented some twelve years earlier. Job interviews with West Coast start-ups, including Fairchild and Shockley Labs, went well until they learned of my familial relationship with the Sprague Electric Company, and subsequent factory visits were summarily cancelled. I did receive job offers from the Hughes Aircraft Thin Film Laboratory in Culver City, California, and the GE Labs in Schenectady, New York, but from a research standpoint the most exciting opportunity was to work with Kurt Lehovec in the Sprague research labs. So, along with our two young sons, John and Bill, my wife and I moved back to the Northeast, and I started work in April 1959. I was the last member of the Sprague family to work for Sprague Electric.

As a researcher in the labs, I had demanding responsibilities. Following studies of silicon surface states with Lehovec, my most rewarding project at Sprague Electric was in 1961, when I headed the small but extremely competent team that developed Sprague's first planar transistor and brought the company into the world of modern semiconductor technology. The team included three German World War II veterans, Dr. Carl Busen, Dr. Hans Scheer, and Dr. Rudolph Dreiner, along with Joseph Lindmayer (a Hungarian refugee and brilliant designer[9]), and Dr. James Casey, a former associate professor at the University of Rhode Island. The resulting SEPT® (silicon epitaxial planar transistor) was available for sampling within a year, and a family of companion ICs or UNICIRCUITS® was ready shortly thereafter. Looking back, the success of these developments was remarkable, considering that Sprague Electric's planar work began from scratch only a year after the process became an industry standard (see Appendix Two).

In the early 1960s, the chairman of my Stanford orals committee, Professor Eric Hutchinson, spent a productive summer in the North Adams labs during which he made two key recommendations: investigate semiconductor doping using ions, and hire one of his former students, Dr. Kenneth Manchester (who was then at Shell Oil), to lead the investigations. Ken did join the company, and in 1964, working with Dr. John MacDougall, filed key patents on ion implantation, a method for introducing impurities into semiconductors that today dominates the integrated circuit industry.

My hands-on research activities lasted only a few years. Although I tried to maintain some personal research, by 1965 I was directing all of Sprague's centralized research and development initiatives. So that I could concentrate on semiconductors, I appointed Dr. Walter J. Bernard, who had been

---

9   J. Lindmayer and C. Y. Wrigley, Fundamentals of Semiconductor Devices (D. Van Nostrand Co., Inc., 1964).

heading the Electrochemical Research Division at Sprague, as my assistant to oversee the R&D in passives. This was a key position, since passive components were generating all the cash and supporting the company as it moved down the semiconductor road.

RESEARCH, DEVELOPMENT, AND ENGINEERING

—

As the 1960s began, R&D investment continued to surge, particularly in semiconductors. In October 1962 a brand new corporate research center was dedicated on Marshall Street, across from the headquarters located in the former Arnold Print Works. Staffed with scientists from all of the basic chemistry and physics disciplines, its mission was to investigate the physical and chemical properties of the materials used in manufacturing both active and passive components, and to create pilot facilities for pre-production of the resultant products. Dr. Fred Fowkes (from Shell Oil) was hired as director of research, and a year later Dr. F. Lincoln ("Linc") Vogel (from RCA) as associate director.

In the semiconductor part of the center, two fully equipped pilot lines were created. The first was for thin film ceramic-based hybrid circuits (CERACIRCUITS®), which were complex circuits with limited volumes, or for where full integration was not yet possible. The second was for development of silicon-based integrated circuits (the previously mentioned UNICIRCUITS®). Initially, as had been done with the SEPT® planar transistor, products developed from both lines were to be transferred to Concord, New Hampshire, for production. However, founder R.C. Sprague had bigger plans.

Left to right: Fred Lack, R.C. Sprague, and Dr. Fred Fowkes in lobby of new research center, c. 1962. Photo courtesy of author

Norton Cushman transferred from the Special Components Division to head the planar pilot facility in the research center, and in 1964 he made a key hire when Dr. Robert S. Pepper, from the University of California at Berkeley, joined the company to accelerate this effort. Besides assuming responsibility for completing the pilot line, Pepper began to build a linear circuit design team that would ultimately be one of the key elements in the Sprague semiconductor turn-around that began in the late 1960s. An outstanding scientist and technician, he also had the ability to hire and retain top-notch talent. In addition, Pepper was a fascinating person. For years, he competitively and very successfully raced hard-track motorcycles, and on more than one Monday morning he arrived for work battered and bruised, especially after one memorable weekend when a missed turn had landed him in a rock quarry. A social visit to his home usually found the living or dining room littered with the parts of one of his dismantled racing machines. In a telephone call several years ago, he commented that by far the best thing that happened to him at Sprague Electric was meeting his second wife, Star, an employee at the Concord, New Hampshire, plant.

At first glance, it seems extraordinary that, in a location as remote as northwestern Massachusetts, Sprague Electric was able to attract so many competent engineers and scientists. This was partly due to the pure beauty of the northern Berkshires, but the company itself offered a number of features that were attractive to top scientists. Sprague had key consulting relationships at major universities such as Stanford, Penn State, MIT, RPI, UConn, and elsewhere. Continuing education was encouraged, and the company supported cooperative programs at the University of New Hampshire (near the Concord and Nashua plants) and North Adams State College (now the Massachusetts College of Liberal Arts, or simply MCLA). In addition, for a while there was a Sprague Electric-Williams College program in which Sprague scientists taught courses in chemistry and physics at Williams, and engineers with only a Bachelor's degree could earn a Master's, studying on a part-time basis. In a few cases, such as that of Dr. Galeb Mahar, who was a Sprague Fellow and later R&D director, the company financially supported an employee's education all the way to a PhD.

JLS: *Before the new research center existed, corporate research, development, and engineering were located in a series of laboratories and offices spread throughout the 87 Marshall Street complex. When I joined the company in 1959, I had a small lab on the third floor of Building 4 (now MASS MoCA's* *famous "Tall Gallery"). Soon my super technician, Howie Marsh, and I were joined by Warren Berner and then Otto Wied. There were other labs full of equipment and offices all around me—part of Kurt Lehovec's blossoming semiconductor research department. Occasionally, I would stop to see my brother, Bob, in human resources just behind the gatehouse, or my father on the second floor in his corner office (which still exists today) on "Mahogany Row." One flight above, Neal Welch and his customer service department functioned as the nerve center, keeping track of everything that was going on both within and outside the company.*

The entrance courtyard was different then. Where visitors now encounter Natalie Jeremijenko's artwork Tree Logic, there stood a building that served as the headquarters of the distributor company, Sprague Products. On the left, there was a tantalum capacitor operation as well as central shipping and receiving. Finally, where the MASS MoCA entrance now opens into a large lobby, there was a spacious cafeteria, open to everyone in the company, where I often ate, although many production and office workers brought their own lunches or went downtown.

While, more than fifty years later, it is impossible for me to remember where everything was in the vast Marshall Street complex, I know I was always impressed by the numerous laboratories, filled with more types of complex equipment than seemed possible in such a relatively small company. There were labs where new materials and devices were created, analytical spaces for testing the makeup of incoming materials (including at times competitors' products), reliability test facilities, and screen rooms for studying interference filter problems, to name just a few.

The largest spaces, though, were the production facilities. Massive chemical machines were used to first etch (in order to increase surface area) and then form (to create the dielectric layer) large rolls of aluminum or tantalum capacitor foil. There, women sat side-by-side in vast rooms at complex rolling machines (many manufactured internally) that created the capacitor sections which were inserted into cans or molded to make the finished product. It always amazed me how the staff could safely operate these complex machines at very high speeds while simultaneously carrying on conversations with their co-workers!

Before moving to Wichita Falls, Texas, the Ceramic Division had its own space in Building 6 at the far western end of 87 Marshall Street, where the two Hoosic River branches converge. Here, great mixers prepared the ceramic materials that were then fired in huge kilns, either as discs or as MLCCs. Seldom visited (and one of the last buildings to be developed by MASS MoCA), this grim space always seemed to have fine ceramic dust filling the air.

During a 1970s Asian trip, Norton Cushman and I had the privilege of a courtesy tour through a Japanese competitor's aluminum capacitor production facility (I believe they hoped to scare us!). They had developed a superior "AC Etch" process which created a much higher aluminum foil etch ratio and volumetric efficiency than Sprague Electric or any US competitor could duplicate. Back in our hotel room, we began to reverse-engineer what we had seen and heard, and a year later Sprague Electric's first pilot AC Etch machine was running in Building 8 (if I remember correctly), on the south side of the inner courtyard along the south branch of the Hoosic.

Sprague Electric reached its peak of employment in North Adams at four thousand in the mid-sixties, but the city's excitement as the center of the Sprague Electric universe was about to change, as the saga of the company's effort to become a major supplier of integrated circuits unfolded.

WORCESTER

—

In 1964, CEO R.C. Sprague decided that Sprague Electric should make a run at becoming a more major force in the integrated circuit market. He recognized that there was already good work under way in the Sprague research center, but believed the process could be accelerated by launching a much larger effort involving a major new facility manned by an experienced team from outside the company. Products from the research center could be transferred in later. After an exhaustive search, Worcester, Massachusetts, was chosen as the location over several seemingly more logical locations, such as Silicon Valley in California. Worcester offered excellent financial incentives, was much closer to North Adams, and was likely to be less prone to the frantic turnover problems of the nascent West Coast semiconductor industry.

Completed in 1966 after an investment of $7 million, the 132,000-square-foot facility, according to company press releases, would "have sufficient capacity to allow Sprague Electric to compete with any of the existing IC suppliers." Since the market potential was huge and growing rapidly, R.C. believed there would always be room for another competent supplier, especially an established component firm with Sprague Electric's gold-plat-

Worcester plant, c. late 1960s
Photo courtesy of author

ed reputation. The route that Sprague initially chose was to be a second-source provider of existing digital logic families—in other words, to produce and market copies of other companies' designs, usually under license. Chosen for early production were DTL (under license from Signetics), RTL (from Fairchild), and TTL (Texas Instruments). There was also a proprietary M514 proximity fuze program. To jump-start this endeavor, the company began interviewing industry veterans to manage the new facility.

Les Hogan came to North Adams to offer his services and those of key members of his Motorola semiconductor team. However, Motorola CEO Bob Galvin was a close personal friend of R.C., and Hogan's apparent lack of loyalty to his current employer nixed any deal. Two years later, Hogan moved on to attempt an unsuccessful rescue of foundering Fairchild.

After several more interviews, John D. Husher was hired from Westinghouse as Sprague's plant manager in Worcester. Husher brought with him a complete operating, technical, and marketing team, numbering (if memory is correct) more than two dozen individuals. Husher saw no need for the North Adams research activities and didn't like reporting to Ken Ishler (then vice president of the semiconductor division). Ishler would eventually be gone, along with Husher, who was even less pleased with the next organizational changes.

Since the capacitor end of the business continued to flourish, not everything of note in Sprague's glory years, leading up to 1966, happened in semiconductors. In 1960, Sprague Electric's image was greatly enhanced by the award of a $1,263,355 contract from the Autonetics Division of North American Aviation to develop components to be used in the Minuteman Missile guidance and control system, with one hundred to one thousand times the reliability of existing devices[10]. The resulting HYREL® solid Ta capacitor not only satisfied the military requirement, but was a key element in the burgeoning computer and data processing market.

In 1962, Sprague Electric had become a Fortune 500 company, and on November 21, 1966, was finally listed on the New York Stock Exchange after its stock had been sold for more than twenty years over the counter. Solid tantalum capacitor sales continued to soar, leading to further expansion in Sanford, Maine, and a new MLCC plant that opened in San Antonio, Texas, to try and boost Sprague Electric's lagging position in this increasingly sizeable segment of the capacitor market.

---

10   Sprague Annual Report, 1960.

Even in capacitors, there was a competitive trend beginning to rear its ugly head, as increased imports of consumer equipment from Japan flooded the market. Radios and televisions were the main end market for aluminum electrolytic capacitors. In testimony before the House Subcommittee on the Impact of Imports and Exports on American Employment, R.C. complained, to no avail, about an unfair market that allowed foreign corporations free access in the United States while they maintained exclusion of American products from their countries. Time would prove how correct he was—his position is still relevant, as markets in India and China continue to be highly protected.

TROUBLE AHEAD: 1967 TO 1976

—

Although 1966 was a record year and there was a modestly upbeat forecast for 1967, clouds were forming in the otherwise sunny skies. With North Adams and Worcester semiconductors going in completely different directions, there was growing concern about the exploding costs of the total semiconductor effort, about where semiconductors were taking the company, and about who was really leading the effort. In early 1967, after decades of intense effort, the International Union of Electrical Workers (IUE) was finally successful in becoming the bargaining agent for the North Adams production workers. The office and technical workers remained under an independent union, at least until 1969 when they became AFTE Local #101 under the AFL-CIO American Federation of Technical Workers. By then, all non-salaried North Adams employees were represented by national unions. Nevertheless, except for the Barre, Vermont, and Visalia, California, plants, the North Adams plants were the only United

States locations ever unionized during the life of the company. Following six months of difficult bargaining, three-year contracts were successfully negotiated in mid-1967, but further severe labor trouble loomed on the horizon.

Instead of growing as forecast, Sprague Electric's revenues dropped to $127 million in 1967 from $142 million in 1966 because of an unexpectedly depressed year for the components industry, although modest profitability was maintained. In 1968, the company recorded its first financial deficit since 1932 ($2.8 million) on revenues of $133 million. After a modest recovery in 1969, disaster struck in 1970 and 1971—largely due to the 1970 strike in North Adams—with combined losses of just under $15 million. (See Table 2, Appendix One.)

Even as revenues dropped, overhead costs still continued to sky-rocket, driven primarily by the Worcester start-up. By the end of 1967, the company's integrated circuits investment had reached $25 million, Worcester employment exceeded nine hundred, and the digital logic second-source strategy had yet to come close to generating sufficient revenue.

JLS: *In August 1967, I was given responsibility for "fixing" semiconductors as senior vice president for semiconductor operations, which included the Concord, New Hampshire, transistor division, the Worcester plant, and the North Adams semiconductor R&D efforts. There were other important corporate changes, as tough insider Neal Welch was named executive vice president, and a new passive manufacturing executive, William E. McLean, joined the company.*

As I became deeply involved in the nuts and bolts of the Worcester operation, I concluded that the second-source strate-

gy was never going to work. In capacitors, Sprague had always been a technology and market leader, usually first to market and therefore enjoying the advantages of early learning-curve costs and pricing. Since my father had started Sprague in 1926 from nothing and succeeded in making it the dominant worldwide passive component company, he was convinced he could do the same in semiconductors. On the other hand, I was just as certain that it was too late to achieve the same dominance and that only a niche strategy, in which the Sprague Semiconductor Group could be a leader, had any chance of success.

The 1968 financial loss served as a wake-up call even as the economic recession eased and sales increased modestly. The quarterly dividend was reduced from fifteen cents to ten cents (and was finally eliminated for good in the third quarter of 1970), and executive vice president Neal Welch moved quickly and forcefully to increase efficiency and reduce costs "using a well-known firm of industrial engineers [the WOFAC Corporation] to introduce more disciplined work practices."[11] Between early 1968 and mid-1969, "VeFAC Programming," the result of classic time-study techniques and supported by onsite "VeFAC Analysts," was introduced throughout the domestic operations. While there were undoubtedly some related savings, the program was expensive and resented by almost everyone, including direct labor operators and overhead personnel. More draconian measures introduced in 1970, such as mandatory salary cuts and layoffs, only added to the overall malaise.

JLS: *I transferred Bob Pepper and his entire technical group to Worcester, leaving only a small materials research team in*

---

11   Sprague Annual Report, 1968.

North Adams reporting to Ken Manchester (who would also move a few years later). Since my own background was mostly technical and I had very limited actual operating experience, I hired industry veteran A. Normand Provost, who had spent the bulk of his business career at Texas Instruments, as Worcester operations manager. Husher resigned, taking with him his entire team, and Norm and I moved quickly to fill the resulting vacancies from both within and outside the company. Worcester and Concord were reorganized as decentralized profit-and-loss centers, as was the chip-and-wire hybrid circuit business unit, now under the direction of John Seacord. Provost also moved quickly to transfer the majority of the expensive "back-end" (assembly and test) operations from Worcester, first to Mexico and then Southeast Asia.

The semiconductor division was still unprofitable, but overall Sprague Electric continued to improve in 1969, with record sales of $147.1 million and modest profitability of $1.46 million. After several dismal years, capacity limitations again loomed, leading to the establishment of new passive component manufacturing plants in Tours, France; Renaix, Belgium; Taiwan; Scotland; and Rheydt, Germany.

JLS: *In the mid-1960s, my wife and I moved into a beautiful home we had built on Laurie Drive in Williamstown, where we expected to live for the rest of our lives. However, to the great disappointment of my entire family, this plan was about to change radically as my father and I met in my study one 1968 fall evening for a quiet discussion about semiconductors. I had decided to move with my family to Holden, a Worcester suburb, after being told flatly by key semiconductor managers that no one would believe I was really committed to the division's success unless I did so. I tried to explain that without* *bankrupting the company, Worcester could only succeed as a niche supplier. Further, I planned to gradually phase out the different digital logic families and bet the future of the division on the ability of Bob Pepper and his linear design team to develop unique linear ICs for consumer and automotive applications. Already in the works were a television color demodulator for Zenith, a sound channel for Delco Radio (the electronics division of General Motors), and a variety of other circuits.*

My father would have none of it, and as the exchange became increasingly heated, he finally called me a coward, someone who was either unable or unwilling to do in semiconductors what he had accomplished in capacitors. This argument came close to ending our relationship forever. Deeply wounded, I quietly told him that he would have to get someone else to run the semiconductor division. Realizing he had gone too far, and that I just might be right, he quickly backed off and then reluctantly capitulated. I received conditional approval for my program, although our relationship would never be quite the same. Still, an awkward parting handshake unexpectedly became a much warmer embrace, and it wouldn't be long before we were united against the opposing forces.

Even as the Sprague Semiconductor Group struggled for its survival, two unexpected events helped brighten the otherwise gloomy outlook.

MOSTEK

—

In the late 1960s, the management of Dallas-based Texas Instruments informed its Metal Oxide Semiconductor (MOS) group that it was moving to Houston. MOS devices had become increasingly important because of their much lower power requirements compared to bipolar. The group rebelled and, led by L. J. Sevin and Lou Sharif, contacted New Business Resources (NBR), a boutique venture capital group in Dallas whose principals, Richard Hanschen and Dr. Richard Petritz, had previously been Texas Instruments executives. NBR next approached Sprague Electric (it is unclear exactly how this contact was made). Thus, in mid-1969, Mostek was born, and for a modest investment of several million dollars Sprague found itself owning just below 50 percent of a promising MOS company with an extremely talented management group and staff.

It was a marriage made in heaven. Sprague had excess capacity in Worcester where Mostek could immediately begin processing Si wafers. Even more notable was Mostek's discovery of Ken Manchester and John MacDougall's experimental single wafer ion implantation reactor in the basement of the North Adams research lab. Initial experiments showed that implantation gave much tighter control of the gate surface potential of a MOS device and therefore superior device performance over any competitor. Convinced of its potential, Mostek bet the company on this new and untried technology. Wafers were initially processed in Worcester, then transported to North Adams for the gate implant, and finally back to Worcester for finishing. The Sprague sales organization helped out with customer contacts. While NBR's Dick Petritz was Mostek's first president, it wasn't long before L. J. Sevin was running the show and the company eventually consolidated its operations in Carrollton, Texas, while continuing to maintain a close relationship with Sprague (its largest stockholder) both in technology and at the management level. In its brief ten-year life as an independent company, Mostek enjoyed phenomenal success, inventing the first single-chip handheld calculator and becoming the early industry leader in the explosive Dynamic Random Access Memory (DRAM) market until Japanese firms became dominant in the late 1970s.

Besides the eventual financial return, Sprague benefited in a number of other ways. Until the move to Texas, Mostek helped cover Worcester's overhead costs, while its success with ion implantation demonstrated that Sprague was a technology leader in semiconductors as well as in passives. More subtly, the personal and business relationships that developed between Sprague and Mostek benefited both organizations. In some ways, the association with Mostek put Sprague Electric on the world semiconductor map.

MOON WAFER
—

In mid-1969, Sprague Electric received an unusual request from NASA for a crash program related to the upcoming July launch of Apollo 11, scheduled to be the United States' first manned landing on the moon. That Sprague Electric should receive such a request was not unusual, since the company had been deeply involved in the US space program since its inception. For example, there were more than fifty thousand Sprague Electric components in every Apollo mission. However, the nature of the request and the timeline required to accomplish the task were anything but usual.

Only a few weeks prior to launch, it was decided that Apollo 11 would leave a time capsule on the moon, and in that capsule would be an artifact containing letters of congratulations from world leaders along with other information, all miniaturized onto

The author and a moon wafer c, 1969
Photo courtesy of author

a single silicon wafer. Within Sprague Electric, the only place such a task could be accomplished was in Worcester, where an adaptation of the basic photolithographic process could place the messages on an oxidized one-and-one-half-inch diameter silicon wafer. Bob Pepper and his technical team were given the task of producing the wafers in an impossibly short period of time. The first messages were received on July 3 and 4, and the first complete wafer (plus spares) delivered back to NASA on July 6. Then, as new messages came in, the whole process had to be repeated. The final wafers, each containing messages from seventy-four heads of state, were picked up by a NASA messenger on July 11. One of them was in place when Apollo 11 was launched on July 16, 1969, and it remains on the moon today. There is a beautiful book by Tahir Rahman, *We Came in Peace for all Mankind*, which describes the Apollo 11 mission and the silicon disc program in detail[12].

Buoyed by the successful completion of this seemingly impossible task (after all, how many companies have a "body part" left on the moon for eternity!), the Worcester group returned to trying to save itself and, in the process, Sprague Electric Company.

THE 1970 STRIKE

—

Operational performance in Worcester continued to improve, and the 1969 Annual Report (published March 5, 1970), glowingly predicted Worcester's profitability in the second half of 1970 (this didn't actually occur until late 1972). There were also

---

12 Tahir Rahman, *We Came In Peace for All Mankind*
    (Leathers Publishing, 2008).

several cautionary warnings: "At this time the outlook for 1970 is clouded by the uncertain general economic climate." "Clouded" proved to be grossly optimistic. The report continued: "Labor contracts with the three unions representing hourly employees in North Adams expired on December 31, 1969, and although negotiations are continuing, at this time no agreements have been reached."

Negotiations dragged on with agonizing slowness through January and into February, 1970. Walter Wood was the chief negotiator for the IUE, while the company was represented by John Winant, Bob Kelley, George Bateman, Bob Sprague Jr., and, mostly behind the scenes, R.C. Sprague. While most of management couldn't imagine that a strike would actually happen after so many years of local prosperity and peace, the company prepared for the worst. Windows were boarded up on Marshall Street to avoid potential damage, a detailed logistics plan was developed to deal with picket lines, and an emergency plan was created to keep some North Adams manufacturing on line using salaried and non-unionized hourly employees. Sprague began to move as much manufacturing as possible out of North Adams, a process that accelerated during the strike itself. This drew a great deal of local criticism, but there was no choice; Sprague Electric had negotiated delivery schedules to its customers. In some cases, these were for products for which the company was the sole source, while others were for essential military and government programs. Inability to meet these commitments for whatever reason could be catastrophic in the short term and cause the long-term loss of key customers as competitors would rush in to fill the void. This is exactly what happened to some of the capacitor lines during the strike, when Sprague lost more than one-third of its market share, a loss from which it took years to recover.

1973 Sprague Electric board of directors; seated left to right: Robert C. Sprague, Augustus B. Kinzel, Bruce R. Carlson, Frederick R. Lack, Jerome B. Wiesner, Ernest L. Ward, Gordon W. Phelps (foreground) Neal W. Welch, and Robert E. Kelley; standing left to right: Robert C. Sprague, Jr., Arthur G. Connolly, John L. Sprague, Jerold R. Zacharias, and Joseph A. Erickson (Robert E. Armitage is absent). Photo courtesy of author

As the negotiating deadline of March 1, 1970, approached, positions on wages and benefits only hardened. On Sunday, March 1, AFTE moved first, voting to strike by a margin of nearly two to one, and picket lines were set up around the Marshall Street complex which the IUE, and nearly all of the other hourly employees, refused to cross. Over the next ten weeks, as management and salaried personnel continued to cross the lines day after day and negotiations stalled, there were increasing incidents of violence; several cars were burned, and there was random heckling, along with pushing and shoving. R.C. was devastated. Despite all his personal courage and toughness, the daily passage across the lines felt to him as if his own family had turned against him.

With little progress, in late April negotiations moved to Washington, DC, under federal mediator J. Curtis Counts, and an agreement was finally reached several weeks later. Wages were to increase by 6 percent the first year of the three-year contract and 5 percent each of the second and third years; there would be other improved benefits in such areas as vacation pay and hospitalization. On the company side, the much-maligned WOFAC Corporation work-study program remained intact, and there was no requirement to bring back the lost jobs. Although the company agreed to general amnesty for the striking workers, North Adams had become a much less attractive place to run a business.

The economic recession only made things worse. Compared to 1969, in 1970 domestic electronic equipment sales decreased 4 percent, and component sales followed suit, dropping 8 percent. In the meantime, component inventories soared to more than a three-month supply. (There is a vicious cycle that continues to plague the electronic components industry to this day, which even sophisticated computer systems haven't been able to prevent: in hard times customers slash their inventories to well below what is appropriate, which only leads to panic-buying and multiple ordering when business improves. Then inventories soar again, and the cycle continues.) The 1970 Annual Report described the situation at the time: "Sprague Electric sales fell more sharply than the overall components industry, reflecting a loss of volume during the ten-week strike as customers, fearing that the strike would spread to non-union plants, took their business elsewhere. [Besides layoffs] there was also an across-the-board salary cut on September 1, 1970, averaging 8 1/2 percent (one half of which was restored January 1, 1971) bringing the break-even point to its lowest level in five years. Some industry improvement is expected in 1971."[13]

Most of what has been written about Sprague Electric relates to the company's labor relations in North Adams and the 1970 strike, when the now nationally affiliated unions representing the office workers (AFTE Local #101) and production workers (IUE) decided it was time to flex their muscles and show the hourly employees just how much they had gained by their new representation. Most of these writings strongly support the unions. However, on a practical level, the strike couldn't have come at a worse time for both management and workers, as the US economy softened.

Why didn't Sprague settle sooner? Wages and benefits in North Adams set the pattern for Sprague Electric operations across the rest of the country, and, in an increasingly competitive market threatened by foreign imports, Sprague just couldn't afford what the unions were demanding, which, in the case of the IUE, was compensation at levels close to those at GE in nearby Pittsfield. From a product-cost basis, what really counted was not how Sprague Electric's hourly wages and benefits compared with GE, which operated in completely different businesses, but how they compared with its competitors' salaries which, according to EIA data, were on the high side in the US and extremely high compared to Asian imports.[14]

Ultimately, both sides lost. Along with a depressed US economy and electronics industry, the strike financially brought the company to its knees. And while the hourly workers received some

---

13   Sprague Annual Report, 1970.

14   Author's personal papers.

improvement in wages and benefits, the strike resulted in an accelerated movement of jobs out of North Adams, to southern facilities with both lower wages and power costs, and to low-wage areas such as Puerto Rico, Malaysia, Taiwan, Hong Kong, and the Philippines. As a direct result of the strike, more than two thousand jobs left North Adams, never to return. It is true that over time many of these jobs would probably have eventually been lost anyway. However, this would have happened at a much more gradual pace and probably without leaving the level of ill will that forever tainted the post-strike relations between management and the North Adams labor unions.

THE AFTERMATH

—

If 1970 was bad, 1971 started out even worse, and component shipments only began to strengthen in the second half. Sprague revenues for the year totaled a dismal $117.9 million, and there was a staggering net loss of $8.1 million. At the operating level, there were further layoffs, and the move toward decentralization accelerated as passive component product development was transferred into the operating divisions, and only a small centralized research activity remained in North Adams. While Worcester continued its strategic shift to linear ICs, and Mostek surged with a broadening product base of calculator chips and DRAMs, Sprague Electric's future in semiconductors was still very much in doubt.

Minutes of an early January 1971 meeting of the executive committee show an increasing panic over the deteriorating financial condition of the company: "There are still too many expense personnel; if we are going to hang in Semiconductors for the future, it will be necessary for the balance of the business to support the activity; we need to immediately reduce weekly overall costs by $150 thousand, primarily by headcount reductions; what are we going to do about the aircraft?" Independent outside director Joseph A. Erickson posed the key question on so many minds, "So what are we going to do about Semiconductors (especially Worcester) where the prospects of making a profit seem poor?"

JLS: *In a private June 23, 1971, memo to my father (it was shared with the executive committee a week later), I argued the Worcester case: "We are making good progress but need more time; some of SEC's greatest talent is in Worcester; we are critical to the success of Mostek; long term the future of the Electronic Components Industry, and therefore Sprague Electric, lies in ICs." I grew up in a home where failure was never an acceptable option, and I had no intention of changing this philosophy in Worcester. I also admit that I had become completely obsessed with saving the business. But I was almost out of time.*

Bruce Carlson countered with a much more conservative plan, which the entire executive committee, except me, endorsed in late July: phase out the Worcester wafer lab; exit all semiconductor product lines except Concord's profitable SEPT® transistors and Worcester's linear ICs; move the linear wafer lab to the North Adams Research Center and related assembly operations to Juarez, Mexico; and sell the Worcester plant.

The lines were drawn, and after an impassioned debate by the full board of directors at its November 23, 1971, meeting, the issue was resolved, at least for the moment, by the following amazingly ambiguous resolution: "Continue, for the time being, without specification as to length of time or degree of intensity, in the IC business, subject to continuing BOD review, and upon condition that the Company take whatever action might be reasonably necessary to maintain its competitive position in its profitable passive component lines." The only negative votes were cast by Arthur G. Connolly (who had completely lost confidence in the current semiconductor initiative) and Bob Sprague Jr. Yet any immediate plan to close Worcester was dropped completely in December because of rapidly increasing IC orders. Like a cat with nine lives, Worcester had bought more time as Sprague Electric's overall business began to surge once more. The semiconductor turn-around climaxed in the fourth quarter of 1972, when, for the first time, Worcester and all semiconductor operations finally turned profitable. However, if R.C. felt he had every right to say "I told you so," it would have to be from a dramatically changed management position.

Responding to heavy pressure from the outside board members, in early November 1971 founder, board chairman, and CEO Robert C. Sprague resigned as head of the company and was elected honorary chairman of the board and chairman of a new executive committee (which also included Welch, Carlson, and Ward). While no longer involved in day-to-day management, R.C. was anything but marginalized, and this executive committee continued to be extremely active until the end of 1976, meeting at least monthly and often weekly.

Reporting on his resignation, a November 10, 1971, article in the The Berkshire Eagle by Thomas Morton summarily dismissed the entire Sprague family: "[over 25 years] Junior's [Robert C. Sprague Jr.] main contribution has [only] been to direct the air arm of the corporate headquarters; John is credited with the Worcester fiasco; and "R.C." has become more infallible than the Pope." However, as they owned nearly 20 percent of the outstanding Sprague Electric shares, it was a little early to write off the Sprague family.

Inside Sprague Electric, there was only one person both acceptable to the board of directors and qualified to succeed R.C. That was Neal Welch who, having joined Sprague Specialties in 1932, knew the company inside and out. If Welch had a blind spot, it was a lack of hands-on manufacturing experience. Still, he had excellent relations with such major customers as IBM, Western Electric, and Delco (known as the "top three" within Sprague Electric), who had to be wooed back following the strike.

There was widespread opinion that Welch would finally terminate the "Worcester experiment," but that didn't happen. Since total company revenue and profitability began to rebound in 1972, then soared in 1973 and 1974 (see Table 2, Appendix One), and Worcester continued to show steady improvement, the issue was dropped—at least until the next disaster.

In order to concentrate resources in only the most profitable product segments, Worcester began a serious program of asset redeployment that included the Worcester-based chip-and-wire Hybrid Circuit operation, which was purchased by Hybrid Systems. Before the sale, this operation had enabled Worcester to pioneer a line of fully integrated power interface circuits. This was the first of an increasingly complex family of power ICs (PICs) that today is one of the major product families of Allegro Microsystems, the successor company of the Sprague Semiconductor Group (see Chapter Six).

Even as Sprague Electric rushed to meet existing requirements, at a meeting of the executive committee on February 26, 1973, market research director Len Lee cautioned that the current growth cycle would probably last only an unusually short two years, at least in part because of expanding imports of home entertainment electronics from Japan. It is unknown whether or not Lee also anticipated the OPEC oil embargo that ran from October 1973 until March 1974, triggering a worldwide recession.[14]

Because of the success of the "Mostek model" (growth by making minority investments in promising high technology start-ups) led by executive committee chairman R.C. Sprague, Sprague Electric made three similar investments between early 1973 and 1975: Boston-based E R Corporation (inexpensive high fidelity audio speakers); Micro-Bit (electron-beam addressable memories); and Princeton Material Sciences (liquid crystal displays for consumer applications). All three had talented management and good ideas, but, unlike Mostek, all three failed, and Sprague had to eventually write off the bulk of its related investments (at a cost of roughly $3 million, not to mention the associated time spent by management and the R&D organization).

In 1974, Sprague Electric had record sales of $214.8 million and nearly record profits of $10.2 million. It was also a year of dramatically changing order patterns, as surging first-half orders dropped dramatically in the second half as the economy slowed and inventories soared. The full financial impact was felt in 1975, when sales dropped to only $161.9 million, causing a loss of $10.3 million. Despite a quick return to profitability in 1976, the dismal financial performance in 1975, coupled with the disasters of 1970 and 1971, led to this being the last year Sprague Electric would enjoy as an independent publicly owned company.

THE THREE MUSKETEERS

—

Coincident with the evolving deterioration in operational and financial performance, three new additions to the board of directors infused new life, new objectivity, broad experience, and new energy into a group that had become almost shell-shocked by the financial roller coaster of the previous years. In February 1974, Dr. David Ragone, dean of engineering at the University of Michigan, joined the board, replacing Jerry Weisner, who had retired. Ragone and R.C. were associates at MITRE. In June, Dr. Robert Charpie, president of the Cabot Corporation and chairman of MITRE, came aboard, replacing the retiring Fred Lack. Finally, in May 1975, Sprague Electric elected its first woman director, MIT associate professor Dr. Margaret MacVicar. Very quickly, these three new directors coalesced as a group, and their collective presence would forever change the direction of Sprague Electric, especially when Charpie began to view Sprague Electric as a possible acquisition candidate for Cabot. In November 1975, Bruce Carlson resigned as president "over differences of opinion on his future role in the company," leaving Welch to wrestle with the full management load while a search committee sought Carlson's replacement from candidates "both inside and outside the Company."[14]

By 1975, there were two very different views of Sprague Electric. In one, the company was a hidden jewel that was successfully reorganizing itself for long-term growth and stability. In the more prevalent view, generally favored by independent stockholders as well as many outside directors, Sprague Electric was a dying company with a failed business model, too many marginal business units, too many facilities, too much overhead, and too many Spragues. While the truth lay somewhere in between, it would take another sixteen years of volatility before Sprague Electric finally succumbed to its continuing problems.

CHAPTER SIX

SPRAGUE ELECTRIC COMPANY (1975–1992)

GK TECHNOLOGIES, PENN CENTRAL, STRUGGLE TO SURVIVE, AND LIFE AFTER DEATH

—

Except for the early start-up years, when ownership was concentrated within the Sprague family and a few family friends, Sprague Electric was a public corporation for most of its life. Ownership, however, was only part of the story. From the beginning to the mid-1970s, R.C. Sprague (regardless of titles, and even during a period of nearly full-time government service) was the chief executive officer and guiding light of the company. His brother, Julian, and his two sons also played significant roles. All this changed in the years following the 1970 strike, as the company struggled to survive. First there was an aborted acquisition (by Cabot Corporation), an actual acquisition (by General Cable/ GK Technologies), a second acquisition (by Penn Central Corporation), a spin-off (as Sprague Technologies, Inc.), and finally the disappearance of the company as a single entity by the early 1990s. In the end, multi-billionaire Carl H. Lindner Jr. had the final say on the demise of Sprague Electric, and was the company's last chief executive officer.

There were actually some very good times before things again began to turn sour in the mid-1980s, and although during much of this period Sprague was well supported by its new owners, the company had lost control of its own destiny. Much like Arnold Print Works before it, Sprague Electric, buffeted by recessionary cycles, increasingly strong foreign competition, and strategic and tactical mistakes, eventually vanished. This chapter discusses what happened, and begins the analysis, to be completed in Chapter Seven, of why the transformation of 87 Marshall Street from an industrial complex to a contemporary art museum is an example of what is happening within much of the US manufacturing sector in the early twenty-first century.

THE BATTLE OVER THE FUTURE OF WORCESTER

—

In mid-1975, following two visits several months apart, new director Dr. Margaret MacVicar circulated a scathing report about the Worcester integrated circuit facility to the outside directors as well as to R.C. Sprague, Neal Welch, Bruce Carlson, and John Sprague. "There is no research and development; general plant-wide consciousness is near zero in regard to vision, materials development, new devices, broad strategy, etc.; where will new ideas come from, who is thinking about them, who has time, is this Division desired and/or viable?"[1]

---

1 Author's personal papers

JLS: *I was seething inside, but all I could do was bite my tongue and reply courteously, as best I could, both in writing and in person. Little else was possible since, after a profitable 1974, my original 1975 sales forecast for the Semiconductor Group (Concord, Worcester, and North Adams Semiconductor R&D) had dropped from a profitable $17.3 million to $12.2 million, well below the break-even point. After-tax profits for the division in 1974 were $634,000 and a negative $1,481,000 in 1975.*

In early September, Dr. MacVicar wrote a second report about Wichita Falls (Sprague Electric's main ceramic capacitor plant in Texas, which was now also my responsibility) that was only slightly more complimentary. "Turnover problems are probably the fault of the plant and not the town; the management talent is the most uneven in regards to quality that I've seen in my limited Sprague plant travels, and the youngest; [still] the plant seems salvageable in the moderate term and not the hopeless situation I had been led to expect."[2]

As it turned out, both her evaluations were wrong. Wichita Falls was never successful and eventually was closed, as AVX and Kemet, and then later several Japanese firms, came to dominate the Multi-Layer Ceramic Capacitor (MLCC) industry. Today, what was originally the Sprague Semiconductor Group is one of the best-kept secret success stories in the semiconductor industry (except to its employees, customers, and competitors). In fact, despite her observations, things began to get really interesting when at least one of the other outside directors, Dr. Robert Charpie, saw a future in Sprague Electric as a whole, as well as possibly in

---

2   Ibid.

semiconductors.

CABOT CORPORATION

—

In the 1975 Sprague Electric Annual Report (published in the spring of 1976) chairman and president Neal Welch reported that "On March 9, 1976, Sprague Electric and the Cabot Corporation agreed in principle to combine the two companies, with Cabot issuing 0.633 of a share of its stock for each share of Sprague, which would become a wholly owned subsidiary of Cabot. On March 3, Dr. Robert Charpie, president of Cabot Corporation, resigned as a director of Sprague Electric to avoid any possible conflict of interest between the two companies."

JLS: *As part of the due diligence, I made visits to several Cabot locations. At the time Cabot had three major businesses: performance chemicals (it is the world's largest producer of carbon black, which is used primarily as a reinforcing agent for rubber in automobile tires), engineered products, and energy. I was impressed with what I saw and the people I met, and everyone seemed friendly, if somewhat reserved. Still, these were very lonely visits, as I just couldn't see how Sprague Electric, the Sprague Semiconductor Group, or I fit into the Cabot plans.*

Then the deal fell apart. "On May 4 it was announced by officers of both Sprague Electric and Cabot that they have, by mutual consent, terminated the previously announced merger negotiations."[3] Why? In one view, it was because R.C. concluded that

---

3 Sprague Electric Annual Report, 1976.

Sprague Electric would not be run the way he felt it should be. Another possible reason could have been reluctance by the Cabot family to have so much Cabot stock in the hands of members of the Sprague family. Anyway, there were no apparent hard feelings, and Charpie rejoined the Sprague board on June 30, 1976, serving as one of R.C.'s closest confidants over the next five months.

Since business and financial results were improving rapidly, and it appeared that Sprague Electric would continue to operate as an independent company, starting in mid-1976 there was a flurry of correspondence, reports, and meetings of the executive committee (Welch, Ward, Ragone, Charpie, and R.C. Sprague, chairman) and the board of directors to discuss the future of the company and its leadership going forward. On June 30, 1976, the board passed a resolution stating preference for an insider to fill the vacancy created by the departure of Bruce Carlson as president.

At an October 18, 1976, executive committee meeting, also attended by the independent outside directors, R.C. proposed a new organizational structure to be in place from November 1976 until November 1979 that included Welch and himself in their current positions, John Sprague as president, and Bill McLean as executive VP. Not pleased, the outside directors asked for more time to consider the proposal, and at least one, Art Connolly, was apoplectic, arguing that John Sprague and Worcester were solely responsible for the company's financial woes since he had assumed responsibility for semiconductors in 1967. At this same meeting, a new name entered the mix as Robert P. Jensen, president of General Cable Corporation, was proposed as a new director.

JLS: *Finally things deteriorated so far that at the end of October 1976 the outside directors requested representation by their own independent counsel, to be paid for by the company. My father and Neal agreed, as long as the sole issue to be discussed was succession to the presidency. In Worcester I followed the proceedings from a distance through periodic input from my father, including blind copies of some of the more contentious correspondence. As the vitriol became increasingly intense, not only did the presidency now seem completely out of reach, I began to wonder if I would even have a job when all the smoke had cleared, or if I really wanted to remain with Sprague Electric as the object of so much ill will. Then the completely unexpected happened.*

GENERAL CABLE/GK TECHNOLOGIES

—

The November 12, 1976, issue of the North Adams Transcript breathlessly reported, "Rumors fly at Sprague as trading in its stock remains suspended at the New York Stock Exchange," and five days later lamented, "The passing of Sprague Electric from the effective control of its founder, Robert C. Sprague, and members of the Sprague family to new ownership marks a major transition in the local industrial scene." The details of the transaction were described in the Sprague Electric 1976 10-K[4]: "General Cable Corporation announced in an Offer to Purchase dated November 12, 1976, and extended to December 6, a tender offer for any and all shares of Common Stock of the company at

---

4   The annual filing that all publicly traded companies must submit to the Securities & Exchange Commission

a price of $19.50 per share." (Prior to the tender, Sprague common shares had been selling at approximately $11 per share.) By March 11, 1977, General Cable had purchased 3,312,745 shares or 95.3 percent of all those outstanding. On December 12, 1976, six of the Sprague Electric independent outside directors (Charpie, Connolly, Kinzel, MacVicar, Ragone, and Zacharias) resigned and were replaced by Robert P. Jensen, Dennis G. Little, Donald R. Kampman, David C. Searls, and Larry G. Morris, all from General Cable, and Hugh H. van Zelm, an investment banker and Florence Sprague's brother. Of the legacy outside directors, only Joseph A. Erickson remained, as his offer to resign was not accepted. The 10-K also reported a dramatic turn-around in Sprague Electric's 1976 financial performance with net sales of $199.6 million, the second highest in the company's fifty-year history, and net income of $6.8 million, compared to a loss of $10.3 million the prior year. Although detailed due diligence by General Cable appears to have been minimal, Bob Jensen's timing was exquisite!

At the December 20, 1976, board of directors meeting, nearly the same management structure that R.C. had unsuccessfully been trying to sell to his original board was put in place for the new General Cable subsidiary, with Neal Welch, chairman and chief executive officer, John Sprague, president and chief operating officer, Bill McLean, executive vice president, and Gerry Tremblay, senior vice president. There was one glaring exception, as Robert C. Sprague finally lost the last of his management responsibilities, although he was elected honorary chairman of the Sprague board of directors. As was his nature, he accepted the change with good grace and took new directions, including supporting the arts, for the remainder of his very full life. He continued to receive honors long after he had withdrawn from the electronics industry, including his February 1985 election to the National Academy of

John L. Sprague and Neal W. Welch c. 1977. Photo courtesy of author

Engineering, the highest professional distinction an engineer can receive in the United States. Thus a new era for Sprague Electric began, an era that would prove to be unusually productive, at least until some of the old problems resurfaced in the mid-1980s.

In the 1976 General Cable annual report, there was a lead photo of a smiling Neal Welch and John Sprague, perhaps both feeling a bit uncomfortable with the new relationship, followed by comments about financial performance, new products, Mostek, overseas operations, and the Sprague Products Distributor subsidiary, which now accounted for roughly one-third of domestic sales. MLC capacitors were once more noted as the dominant future capacitor family, and Worcester continued to successfully refine a strategy built around specific, mostly niche areas of product lead-

Robert P. Jensen. Photo courtesy of author

ership, including linear consumer ICs, high-voltage, high-power interface circuits for computer and printer applications, and Hall Cell ICs for automotive applications. The recovery from the 1975 debacle was breathtaking. Compared to 1976, by 1980 sales had more than doubled to $453 million, and operating income increased nearly six times to $77.6 million.

Often when such mergers or acquisitions occur, the acquirer immediately starts to impose its culture on the acquired company, consolidates similar functions to reduce costs, appoints members of its management team to key positions, and thus all too often destroys what was best about the purchased entity. This did not happen with General Cable; it wasn't the way chairman Bob Jensen worked. He had acquired a going concern that he expected would continue to run its own show—at least as long as it continued to meet its commitments. In 1977, Sprague Electric contributed 37 percent of General Cable's consolidated sales and nearly 44 percent of its operating income; by 1980, the equivalent numbers were 38 percent and nearly 52 percent of what was now called GK Technologies, and which included another acquisition, Automation Industries.

JLS: *Jensen was an excellent manager, very demanding but also fair. He did have a quick temper and, a big man physically, at times used his size to intimidate others. He always carried a large briefcase which everyone assumed must be filled with volumes of important papers. I learned otherwise at a Mostek board meeting when we had to briefly share a bedroom due to a mix-up in the motel reservations. Jensen popped open the briefcase which, it turned out, was filled with huge Cuban cigars, one of which he immediately lit. Luckily, I was later able to escape to another room!*

Overall relations between Welch and Jensen were amicable, and Welch worked hard to keep it so. Inevitably, however, problems did arise. On one memorable occasion, a major customer called Jensen directly when one of its production lines was shut down by delinquent Sprague deliveries. Furious, Jensen exploded at Welch, and on the spot threatened to replace him with John Sprague. He cooled down quickly upon learning that the problem was primarily caused by an unexpected dramatic increase in the customer's delivery requirements, and that everything was being done to increase capacity. However, Welch was shattered by Jensen's reaction, especially since the acquisition of Sprague Electric was beginning to make Jensen look like a genius.

JLS: *Neal and I had worked well together for years, although* *the relationship always remained a bit prickly. He was "old Sprague," conservative, and above all oriented toward the passives side of the business and keeping the customer happy, whatever the cost. I was "new Sprague," much younger, semi-conductor-trained and more of a risk-taker. It was never clear if Welch agreed with the semiconductor initiative, and when I once asked him how he felt I was doing, he replied, "You are a good planner," certainly a less than ringing endorsement. Still, in the late 1970s we produced outstanding results as a team.*

While Sprague management struggled to keep up with the resurgent customer requirements, the company began to reevaluate its relationship with Mostek. While the subsidiary continued to perform admirably, there were danger signals on the horizon, especially in the key DRAM (Dynamic Random Access Memory) business, in which Japanese semiconductor companies were beginning a successful assault on the US industry. Concerned about Mostek's future, and needing cash to support Sprague's skyrocketing capital requirements, in 1978 Sprague Electric sold 600,000 Mostek shares for $9.8 million, reducing its ownership from 34 to 21 percent. The following year, Sprague sold the remainder for $51.5 million.

In 1979, United Technologies purchased Mostek for $345 million and then completely mismanaged the acquisition, eventually selling what was left of the company to Thomson Semiconductor for $71 million in 1985. In the meantime, key Mostek executives had gone on to other distinguished careers, with L. J. Sevin joining Ben Rosen in 1981 to form Sevin Rosen Funds; Vin Prothro founding Dallas Semiconductor in 1984; and Bob Palmer joining Digital Equipment in 1985 and replacing founder Ken Olsen as CEO in 1992.

R.C. Sprague was no longer directly involved in the business or industry when, in April 1979, he received probably his most weighty accolade, becoming the only two-time recipient of the Electronic Industries Association's Medal of Honor. The following year he seemed even more pleased when another of his goals was finally realized. At a December 19, 1980, special meeting of the Sprague Electric board of directors, John Sprague succeeded Neal Welch as CEO through a change in the by-laws that added this responsibility to that of the president. Welch continued as chairman, at least for the moment. However, once again change was in the works.

Early in 1981, Jensen announced that "discussions with Penn Central Corporation (PCC) have culminated in an offer by Penn Central to purchase for cash GK Common at $50/share and Convertible Stock at $59.50 resulting in GK becoming a wholly owned subsidiary of PCC. We expect that after the merger the Company will continue under present management and organization as a subsidiary of PCC."[5] The purchase price of $704 million was $175 million greater than the asset value of GK Technologies. The offer was accepted by the GK board on February 23. Within Sprague Electric there was almost universal shock: "Penn Central, the bankrupt railroad company, what does it know about electronic components?" As it turned out, not much!

PENN CENTRAL CORPORATION

—

The Penn Central Corporation resulted from the 1968 merger of the two largest US railroads, the Pennsylvania and New York

---

5   GK Technologies Annual Report, 1980.

Central, both with roots going back to the early 1800s. When Penn Central filed for bankruptcy in 1970, it was the largest corporate failure in American history. After years of litigation, in January 1981 Penn Central received cash compensation of $2.1 billion from the US government for its rail properties, which became part of federally funded Conrail in 1976. Now flush with cash and a $2.2 billion tax loss carried forward, what had once been a bankrupt company was very rich, and it quickly embarked on a major acquisition program. One of the biggest purchases was Marathon Manufacturing, a maker of offshore oil-drilling platforms and several other energy-related businesses acquired in 1979. Other parts of Penn Central included its Living and Leisure Group (Arvida, Great Southwest, and Six Flags Corporations) and the Diversified Industries Group.[6] There seemed to be no strategic fit in such an eclectic mix.

Although seemingly now buried in the corporate structure of a highly diversified more than $3 billion corporation, Sprague was still prominently featured in the early rhetoric concerning the GK acquisition: "One of GK's primary businesses is conducted by Sprague Electric Company. Sprague is one of the world's leading manufacturers of capacitors, a vital component used in almost all types of electronic equipment sold around the world." Despite recessionary pressures in the 1981 economy causing a decrease in Sprague's income, it was predicted that "a recovery in the domestic economy during 1982 should result in improvement for all operations and the longer-term forecast for electronic components continues bright."[7]

---

6   See, for example, fundinguniverse.com.

7   Penn Central Corporation (PCC) Annual Report, 1981, pp. 16–20.

Still, the drop in earnings was the first since 1976; after five consecutive years of improved performance—and based on Sprague Electric's history of cyclical performance—this should have served as an early warning that the electronic component industry was probably approaching another of its recessionary cycles. However, no one seemed worried.

The top management of Penn Central also changed, as Al Martinelli, previously president and CEO of the Penn Central Energy Group, replaced Richard Dicker as president and CEO. There were two new additions to the board of directors who would have a profound impact on the future direction of the company: Carl H. Lindner Jr., a brilliant self-made Cincinnati billionaire and CEO of American Financial Corporation, and his right-hand man, Ron Walker. By 1983, Lindner had accumulated sufficient stock to take control of Penn Central and assume chairmanship of its board.

Jensen moved on to Tiger International, where he was elected chairman and CEO in 1985. Within Penn Central, Gene Swartz moved up to fill the vacancy left by Jensen as president of the Electronics, Defense and Telecommunications Group, thus becoming John Sprague's new boss. As the result of all these changes, Sprague, at a time when it could least afford it, was now embedded in an initially supportive organization with good intentions, but minimal experience in the components industry and—in the case of Lindner and Walker—little desire to be there.

At an early presentation to Lindner's board, Sprague management sought financial support for a much-needed expansion and upgrade of its silicon wafer processing facility in Worcester. Director Ron Walker initiated the discussion by commenting, "Well, gentlemen, we have already spent a lot of money on your company, so I assume that in the future no more will be required." Upon hearing that the overall costs of expansion in Sprague Electric were such that it would be impossible to finance them without additional support from the parent corporation, Walker grumbled, "What a terrible business!" Not a good start! [8]

The Worcester needs were eventually filled by two expansions of the original facility and the 1984 acquisition of Solid State Scientific (SSSI) in Willow Grove, Pennsylvania. The Solid State acquisition proved a poor solution that would haunt the company for years. Even after detailed due diligence by Sprague technical and marketing personnel had concluded that SSSI would do little to either solve the capacity requirements or add appreciable new revenue, Penn Central management insisted on completing the acquisition. So Sprague reluctantly agreed, sending Peter Loconto, the Worcester operations manager, to try to improve the unit. Performance improved, but the losses continued for years.

JLS: *At a several-day management meeting in one of PCC's Florida properties, I had the unenviable assignment of telling the Sprague Electric story as the last presenter on the Friday afternoon agenda. For two days, we had been sitting in a darkened conference room listening to hour after hour of mostly boring presentations. Outside, you could hear the surf breaking and smell the salt spray from the ocean, although there was little opportunity to enjoy any of it. When it was finally my turn to try and make electronic components sound exciting, I could hear snores in the back of the room. No one seemed interested. There were no questions, but as I walked out with the rest of the crowd, Carl Lindner commented, "Good job."*

---

8   Author's recollection of the meeting.

During a later corporate Christmas party we were seated next to each other. For all his wealth and success, Lindner was a deceptively mild-looking man, tall and distinguished with white hair, glasses, and a friendly smile. He often wore white suits and enjoyed driving around his Florida holdings in one of his fleet of yellow Stutz Bearcats. Conversation was difficult until Lindner learned that I was on the board of Worcester-based State Mutual Life Assurance Company of America. In the lively discussion that ensued, it became apparent that Carl strongly favored businesses that had predictable sales and earnings, were non-cyclical, non-capital-intensive, and weren't technology-based, the antithesis of Sprague Electric. Later he asked, "John, do you know what I am?" Sensing I didn't know how to reply, he leaned forward and smiled, "John, I am the lender of last resort." I wasn't exactly sure what that meant, but assumed it translated into something like, "Buy low, sell high!" Unfortunately, Sprague Electric didn't seem to fit that formula very well.

The forecast improvement in the economy did not occur in 1982 or even early 1983, as the severe 1981 economic recession dragged on. Then, with inventories at a dangerously low level, 1984 component orders surged, and Sprague Electric scrambled to catch up with the delayed demand. Unfortunately, the surge was short lived as the economy slowed again in 1985. It couldn't have happened at a worse time. Sprague Electric was in the middle of an aggressive and expensive expansion program just as sales dropped off a cliff. As shown in Table 3 in Appendix One, as profitable as the latter half of the 1970s had been, the mid-1980s were a disaster. The cyclicality of the electronic components industry requires a business model in which fixed costs are maintained at a level that allows financial survival during the inevitable down cycles. However, following the extraordinary last half of the 1970s and urged on by Penn Central, Sprague Electric continued to add fixed costs as if the good days would never end.

As Sprague Electric continued to decentralize corporate functions, move manufacturing to lower- cost locations, and consolidate plants where it made sense, the future of North Adams as corporate headquarters became increasingly questionable. Sprague's employment had steadily declined from a peak of more than four thousand in 1966. Following the 1970 labor stoppage, it dropped to just over two thousand, and by 1982 was down to fifteen hundred. However, it was a spring 1983 Penn Central corporate visit to North Adams that sealed the city's fate.

The North Adams Harriman-West Airport has a single paved runway and lights, but no tower, and, sitting at the base of Mount Williams, is subject to swirling wind turbulence. Its 4,300-foot length (it may have been shorter in the early 1980s) is adequate for handling jet aircraft, but, even under good weather conditions, landing there can be challenging. So one can imagine the anxiety of the passengers—a full load of Penn Central directors and executives—when they flew into the valley on the Penn Central jet to land on what must have looked like a postage stamp.

This was a first-time visit to North Adams for many of them. As the cavalcade of shaken executives drove from the airport to downtown North Adams, they noticed the numerous old, often empty, textile mills along Route 2. Upon entering the gates of the 87 Marshall Street complex, they were escorted to the beautiful main conference room, with its massive oak table covered with tan felt, where the Sprague Electric senior executives and board of directors welcomed them. Following cordial introductions, a limited number of presentations, and a brief tour (it appears that

Sprague Electric Lexington corporate headquarters.
Photo courtesy of author

lunch was skipped), the visitors rushed back to the airport, happy to be gone and hopeful that the Penn Central jet had enough power to take off and clear the surrounding hills.

The feedback from Penn Central CEO Martinelli was swift and unequivocal. To paraphrase, "I'm never going to fly into that airport again. North Adams is no place for the headquarters of our highest technology investment. Get headquarters out of there to somewhere appropriate, such as the Route 128 area of Boston." Thus began the planning of a new world headquarters in Lexington, Massachusetts, restructuring of the Sprague board of directors and management, and an unacceptably expensive initiative called Actions for Profitable Growth (APG).

APG was announced in early 1984 after nearly a year of detailed planning by the Penn Central Strategic Management and Planning Group, Gene Swartz, and Sprague management. It set seemingly impossible goals of reaching net sales of $1 billion and pretax earnings of $100 million by 1987. This meant rapid expansion of the existing Sprague Electric product lines and probably strategic acquisitions as well. The only possible way such a plan could succeed was if the electronic component market enjoyed another steady growth period similar to the latter half of the 1970s. It didn't.

Full occupancy and the formal dedication of Sprague's world headquarters at 92 Hayden Avenue in Lexington didn't occur until December 4, 1984, but personnel transfers and hiring began mid-year. In announcing plans for relocating headquarters to Lexington in early 1984, CEO John Sprague said that related transfers from North Adams would total only about a dozen people. However, when all was said and done, the consolidation of most corporate functions in Lexington and in a new distribution facility in Mansfield, Massachusetts, coupled with acceleration of the corporation-wide decentralization process, led to an actual loss of more than 550 hourly and salaried jobs in North Adams over the next several years. The company badly mishandled communicating the actual job-loss numbers, so that when the new number was finally released in October 1984, the news stunned and infuriated the North Adams community, Sprague Electric's North Adams employees, and new mayor John Barrett, creating a feeling of betrayal that exists to this day. More than twenty-five hundred Sprague jobs had already left between 1970 and 1984 (the majority resulting from the strike), and although some lingering manufacturing would remain in North Adams, Sprague was now perceived as having abandoned the city that had helped make it great. In actuality, by mid-1987 there were still some 640 Sprague jobs in North Adams, mostly in filters, wet and foil tantalums, and at Commonwealth Sprague on Brown Street, meaning that Sprague Electric was still the second largest Berkshire County employer (excluding General Electric in Pittsfield), behind Williams College (with 830)[9]. Unfortunately, by 2000, eight years after Sprague Electric no longer existed as an entity, most of the remaining jobs were also gone.

The new headquarters was located at the intersection of Routes 2 and 128, west of Boston, and the facility was a beauty. A two-story former Burroughs office building was completely gutted and rebuilt from the bottom up. The building was gray brick and glass and included a wide second-story recessed balcony overlooking Route 2. Sprague Electric had finally gone big-time, at least as far as Penn Central was concerned.

JLS: *Looking back, while the move from North Adams seemed to make sense for a soon-to-be billion dollar company, it made less sense considering the related upheaval of key personnel, especially when viewed strictly from a cost standpoint. Consolidation in the research center, or in a new facility in North Adams's Hardman Industrial Park, had been briefly considered by the planning group, but quickly abandoned since labor problems would remain, and Penn Central management clearly preferred a metropolitan location. Ironically, less than three years later the new headquarters facility in Lexington would also be closed, and there would be a new company, Sprague Technologies, Inc., with new headquarters in Stamford, Connecticut, and a new CEO.*

JLS: *Nonetheless, everything was upbeat at the dedication of*

---

9   *Berkshire Eagle*, June 18, 1987. The third largest employer was the North Adams Regional Hospital with 500 employees.

the new headquarters as I addressed the invited guests. "With the support of PCC we have formulated a far-reaching accelerated growth plan having a goal of $1 billion in sales by 1987. Current 1984 estimates indicate we will reach record sales in excess of $500 million (the actual was $571 million), and we are confident that we can reach our ambitious goal for 1987." Al Martinelli followed by describing Sprague Electric as the "flagship of the Penn Central Company."

I also described my new, highly decentralized organization built around a group of worldwide product managers or WWPMs, with full worldwide profit and loss responsibility for their product groups. Reporting directly to me in Lexington were Sprague Electric veteran executive VP Don McGuiness (operations), John Murphy (SVP, technology and support), and Fred Windover (VP and chief counsel), along with newcomers Jack Darcy (SVP, marketing and sales), Larry Switzer (SVP, finance and administration), and Doug Smith (planning). I also introduced the new WWPMs, all seasoned Sprague Electric executives: Tom Browne (aluminums and thick film networks), Peter Loconto (ICs), Peter Maden (tantalums), Hal Mahar (special components), Bill Milton (ceramics), and Jim Sherry (films). Yet what seemed so logical and clean on paper turned out to be far less effective in reality.

The problems began in Lexington, where I was never able to create a cohesive team, primarily because there were too many personal agendas. Although his aggressive and profane persona rubbed some of the older Sprague sales veterans the wrong way, Jack Darcy and I hit it off immediately and he brought a wealth of experience, especially in the electronic distribution industry. Switzer was a different matter. A former Iowa State football standout, Larry is a big man, both figuratively and physically. It quickly became apparent that what he really wanted was my job and the sooner the better. After I learned that he had taken his case directly to Penn Central management, Larry was quickly gone and, following several interim appointments, replaced by Sprague veteran Don Christiansen.

All the WWPMs reported directly to Don McGuiness, making him the clear number two man in the company. He had done an outstanding job in semiconductors, but, feeling his oats, shortly after his promotion he told me that it was time for me to step aside, become a figurehead, and let him run the show. Since I had no intention of retiring, relations between us quickly soured. However, there was an even more serious problem. Don was a firm disciple of EST (Erhard Seminars Training, which claimed "to transform one's ability to experience living") and insisted that his new subordinates also embrace the discipline. Most objected, and after a year Don was gone, and I chose to personally assume his operating responsibilities.

As one might expect, not all WWPMs were created equal. Peter Maden was particularly effective, in no small part because he was responsible for solid tantalums, one of the few capacitor families for which Sprague Electric had been able to maintain worldwide market leadership since its invention by Sprague in the early 1950s. The others were competent, although over time Tom Browne's efforts at self-promotion became an increasing problem for me.

Even if Lexington had operated perfectly, it probably would have changed the outcome only marginally. For nearly ten years, through up-and-down market cycles, expansions and contractions, and changes in management and organization, Sprague Electric had operated successfully. Semiconductors had finally become an important asset rather than a liability, and after five extraordinarily successful years during the latter part of the 1970s, even during the downturn which followed from 1981 through 1984, Sprague had maintained solid profitability. Then came the failure of the "Actions for Profitable Growth" business model.

Hindsight is easy. Yet, thinking back some twenty-five years later, as expenses soared I knew what we were doing was wrong. Even though the move from North Adams made long-term sense, at the time we just couldn't afford it. The same was true with APG. Instead of trying to grow everything, we should have concentrated on those businesses in which we excelled or in which we believed we had to succeed. And yet knowing this, I chose to embrace and proceed with the plan. It was as if I was on a train platform, the express was about to leave, and if I didn't climb aboard I would be left behind. There was also an evolving competitive factor. Starting with consumer electronics—a key market for many Sprague Electric product families, including ICs and aluminum capacitors—Japanese corporations were becoming formidable worldwide competitors. Additionally, they were starting to seize control of the multi-layer ceramic capacitor industry. So as offshore competition intensified, increasingly tantalum capacitors were the only dielectric family in which Sprague Electric continued to maintain a leadership position.

While Table 3 in Appendix One tells the overall story, there were significant subplots. The year-to-year volatility of revenues was driven primarily by economic cycles. For example, the brief 1984 surge in component requirements was quickly followed in 1985 by a plunge in incoming orders and revenues. Then there was IBM, the company's largest and most valuable customer for much of its life. Unfortunately, there was a glaring problem in doing business with the world's largest computer manufacturer—IBM's apparent inability to accurately forecast its component requirements and control its inventories during the inevitable economic cycles that continued to plague the electronics industry, despite its overall dramatic growth. In up markets, Sprague was pushed to the limit to meet IBM's surging requirements, only to face sudden unexpected cancellations when the economy dropped. The solid tantalum and networks business units were particularly savaged by this problem.

The overall financial losses in 1985 and 1986 were clearly unacceptable. On the operating side they were the combined result of both lower revenues and the added overhead costs related to Lexington and the APG initiative. However, the largest problem didn't stem from operating losses, but rather was the result of restructuring costs and reserves, the details of which are, unfortunately unknown today. Not surprisingly, growth at any cost quickly shifted to a fight for survival.

Penn Central brought McKinsey & Company into Lexington to "help," and after an inordinately expensive year on site, the consulting firm concluded that the sum of Sprague Electric's business units as individual entities was worth more than the company as a whole. In other words, McKinsey recommended breaking up the company and selling off the pieces.

JLS: *While the agony of downsizing was consuming the company in 1985 and 1986, I attempted to visit every worldwide location that was being closed to try and explain why. In hindsight, I clearly failed to do this effectively in North Adams. It was a dreadful task because at stake were not just bricks and mortar, but people's lives. Between 1984 and 1987, Sprague's* *worldwide employment dropped from over 12,000 to 8,400. On one occasion, I wasn't sure I would get out alive after addressing the angry employees of an about-to-be-closed plant in West Germany.*

SPRAGUE TECHNOLOGIES, INC. (STI)

—

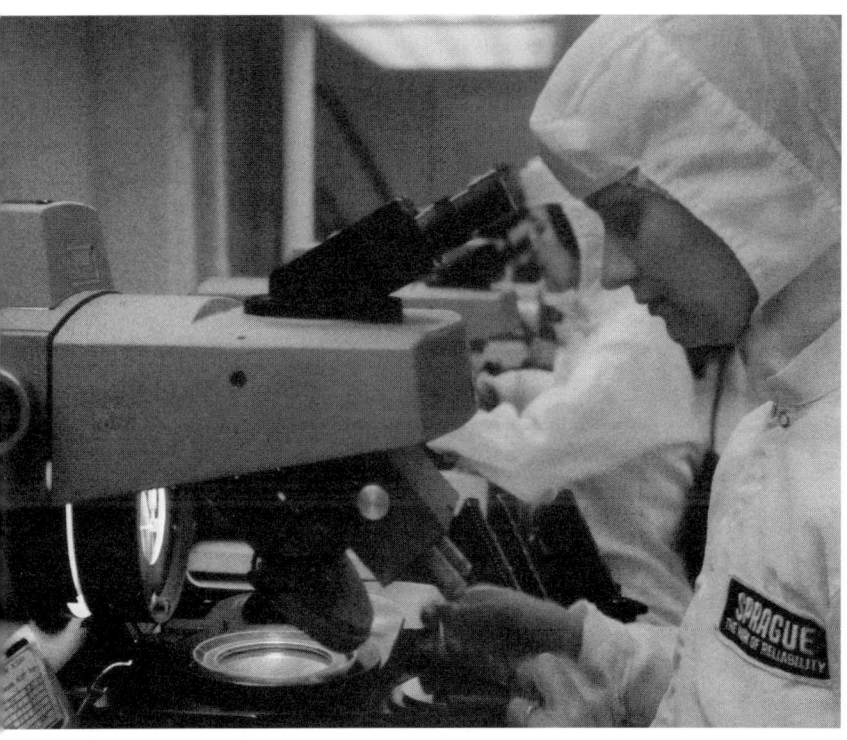

Worcester integrated circuit wafer fab c. mid-1980s.
Photo courtesy of author

Analysis of the individual Sprague Electric business units in 1985 and 1986 shows the problems that Sprague was facing. The operating losses were concentrated in Solid State Scientific, Aluminums (in 1985), and MLCCs. In Sprague's core fixed-capacitor segment, only tantalum capacitors, both Solids and Wet & Foils, showed continuing major profitability potential. Networks, which are used primarily in computer applications, also showed promise. However, as previously noted, the extreme volatility in the order patterns of IBM was a major risk here as well. It is notable that, during these two terrible years, Worcester ICs and Concord discrete semiconductors both remained modestly profitable.

By 1986, Carl Lindner had assumed complete control of Penn Central. Now CEO as well as chairman, he had quickly eliminated most of the prior Penn Central management, and moved the PCC headquarters to his home city of Cincinnati. As he continued to re-deploy and shed parts, he created Sprague Technologies, Inc. with former Penn Central executive vice president and chief financial officer Ed Kosnik as CEO. Initially, Lindner put in place a two-layer corporate structure in which John Sprague continued as president of Sprague Electric, but now reported to Kosnik. Such a one-on-one structure made no sense except as a short-term expedient.

JLS: *In early 1987 our family suffered two overwhelming personal tragedies. On April 10 my brother, Bob, died in a fiery crash at the North Adams Harriman-West Airport. Unable to deal with the loss of her elder son, my mother died of heart failure only two short months later, on June 1. My father grieved, but his indomitable spirit was not broken by these twin tragedies. As was his nature, rather than lament these losses and the dismantling of the company he had founded, he chose to enjoy his remaining family—which at the time includ-*

ed eight grandchildren and eight great-grandchildren—along with his other interests, such as the Elm Tree Foundation and especially the Williamstown Theatre Festival, both of which he helped found. He lived another four years and died peacefully in his sleep at home in Williamstown on September 28, 1991.

In August 1987, Lindner spun off Sprague Technologies to the Penn Central stockholders as a separate company. However, the company was hardly independent. The board of directors was a group of Penn Central loyalists; Lindner was its chairman, and he controlled more than one third of its stock. Sprague was now just another pawn on an ever-changing chess board, and its fate was entirely in Lindner's hands. It soon became clear that what he wanted was to exit all of Penn Central's manufacturing businesses, including Sprague Electric, and use the generated cash to expand his property and casualty insurance interests.

STI started well by returning to modest profitability with net income of $3.6 million on sales of $437 million. Although Penn Central was no longer available as its bank, Kosnik reassured stockholders that "internally generated funds [plus a recently negotiated $40 million revolving line of credit] should be sufficient to support STI's needs in the short term."[10] But following another market collapse that began in late 1987, trouble was again on the way.

JLS: *At a well-attended spring 1987 sales meeting on Cape Cod, which also included spouses, Kosnik celebrated a "new beginning" for the sixty-year-old Sprague Electric Company. Despite still being titular president, my sole responsibility*

---

10   STI Annual Report, 1987, p. 17.

was to present an abbreviated history of Sprague Electric. In the middle of my talk, I became suddenly and uncontrollably emotionally overcome by what was happening to the company founded by my father and where I had worked for twenty-eight years. I had a strange out-of-body experience, during which I was standing in the corner watching myself at the podium, hearing the shocked audience reaction and my wife's strangled "Oh, John," and noting that Kosnik, seemingly unmoved, was staring stonily straight ahead. Chagrined and embarrassed, I recovered quickly and, after apologizing, was able to finish my talk without further incident. On the way out, several well-wishers stopped to tell me I had no reason to apologize. Nevertheless, I had given Penn Central the opening it needed.

Only weeks later I was given my walking papers: "John, it is clear that you just aren't with the new program." I was in no position to argue, and anyway felt the offered severance package was more than fair. It included a position as vice chairman of the new Sprague Technologies board (Lindner was chairman), an office and consulting assignment in Worcester for a year (a difficult arrangement, to say the least, for semiconductor WWPM Dick Morrison), and help in creating a consulting company, John L. Sprague Associates, which was incorporated on April 15, 1988, "to provide consulting services to technology-based firms."

As the only associate, for the next twenty years I enjoyed a number of interesting consulting relationships, including lengthy ones with ALCAN, AMP, and RAYCHEM. I also served on numerous boards, including two small semiconductor companies, Sipex (now part of Exar) and California Micro Devices (now part of ON Semiconductor), and one capacitor company, Aerovox Corporation, headquartered in New Bedford, Massa-

chusetts. Today, I am an amateur historian and keep an office at MRA Labs in Adams, a small ceramic materials company started by Dr. Galeb Maher in 1990 as a spin-off of what remained of the Sprague Electric R&D laboratories. But what happened to Sprague Technologies, Inc.? It started bravely, but by 1992 it too was gone.

For the whole of 1988, STI had net income of $13.2 million on sales of $505 million. But the improvement over 1987 occurred entirely in the first six months as the recession finally caught up with the electronics industry mid-year, a deep recession that would drag on into the early 1990s. Internally, the search began again for a new exit strategy. Merger discussions started with AVX, Kemet, and several other potential partners, but to no avail. Preparing for a probable separation into two companies, for the first time Sprague reported results by product segment: components (basically all the non-semiconductor products) and semiconductors. The former had 1988 sales of $386.5 million and operating income of $29 million, while semiconductors (including Solid State Scientific) broke even on sales of $118.1 million. For STI as a whole, profits continued to be dominated by solid tantalum capacitors. Still, as summarized in Table 4 of Appendix One, STI was heading into a classic downturn similar to the one that had just concluded.

As the recession continued into 1989 with no improvement in sight, STI was back to restructuring and moving towards being solely a passive component company. Revenue of $344 million led to a loss of just under $100 million, of which $80 million was another restructuring reserve. All business units, including solid tantalums, were savaged by a $40 million IBM shortfall, once more caused by massive excess inventories at the customer level. Only the tantalum department was able to eke out a modest profit. MLCCs, Fil-Mag, semiconductors, and several other small business units were discontinued, while capital expenditures were limited almost entirely to surface mount technology (the growing trend in device packaging) for networks and solid tantalums. Considering the nearly $100 million 1989 restructuring reserve, at first glance 1990 sales of $315 million and a loss of $49 million looks even worse, but actually things seemed to be looking up now that STI was a supplier of only tantalum and aluminum capacitors and thick film networks. On December 19, 1990, the semiconductor business was sold to Sanken Electric Ltd. of Japan (and renamed Allegro MicroSystems) for $61.9 million in cash, versus a book value of $106 million. Therefore the STI loss for the year was almost all due to the book loss on this transaction. With all bank offerings repaid, cash and equivalents of nearly $33 million, and a $160 million tax-loss carry-forward, Kosnik reported that, despite the continuing recessionary environment, STI was now well positioned for future growth and profitability. However, in an absolutely stunning reversal, STI died completely in 1991, although burial wasn't until 1992,

Kosnik's 1991 STI annual report message changed dramatically from 1990: "In recent years Sprague divested unprofitable business units in attempting to create a profitable core component business. Despite downsizing, the company was unable to produce consistent profitability as the industry matured and the component recession lingered. The divestitures culminated with the sale of the Tantalum Capacitor and US Thick Film Network businesses in February 1992 [to Vishay Intertechnology, Inc., for $120 million in cash plus 'certain other considerations']. With the sale the company has effectively exited electronic component manufacturing."

On April 17, 1992, the STI board of directors elected Carl Lindner to the additional post of CEO, replacing Ed Kosnik. Sale or closure of several businesses was still to be accomplished. However, all that remained of Sprague Electric was a modest pile of approximately $100 million in cash and a tax-loss carry-forward in the range of $130 million. Adding this to what had already been accumulated within Penn Central by the prior sale of other businesses, Lindner continued the transformation of Penn Central into an insurance company, which in 1994 was renamed American Premier Underwriters, Inc.[11]

If Sprague Electric no longer exists today as an entity, successors to its different business units and operations are spread around the world. These include the previously mentioned MRA Labs; two specialty private film capacitor companies, SBE, Inc. in Barre, Vermont, and Dearborn Electronics in Longwood, Florida; and a private aluminum capacitor company, Barker Microfarads in Hillsville, Virginia. United Chemi-Con also continues to operate the former Sprague aluminum capacitor plant in Lansing, North Carolina. All proudly acknowledge their Sprague Electric heritage.

Succeeding where Sprague had failed, Vishay Intertechnology, Inc., with revenues in excess of $2 billion and more than twenty-two thousand employees worldwide, is today one of the world's largest suppliers of passive components, while also marketing a limited offering of semiconductor devices. Founder and CEO Dr. Felix Zandman, who died in June 2011, grew Vishay primarily through the acquisition of existing businesses and product lines, rather than internal research and development. When Vishay purchased the Sprague tantalum capacitor busi-

---

11   Multiple online sources, including fundinguniverse.com.

nesses in 1992, Zandman immediately started to move much of the solid tantalum production to Israel to take advantage of its lower labor rates—at least compared to the United States and Europe—and high work ethic. Additionally, Zandman was successful in negotiating very attractive tax incentives with the Israeli government[12]. He also purchased the Sprague trade name, and today one can purchase a broad line of Vishay-Sprague capacitors, dominated by the solid tantalum surface mount configuration that Sprague had pioneered prior to the acquisition. Wet and foil tantalums, plus some solids, were consolidated in Sprague's former Sanford, Maine, plant, leading to major job losses in Concord, New Hampshire, and Tours, France. Using market share as a measure, these moves have apparently not been completely successful. Prior to the acquisition, Sprague and Kemet each shared roughly 25 percent of the world tantalum capacitor market. According to a Paumanok Publications, Inc. report in March 2008, Vishay's tantalum share had slipped to 10 percent, behind AVX, Kemet, and NEC/TOKIN.

The other Sprague business that has succeeded admirably is Allegro MicroSystems, the former Worcester-based Sprague Semiconductor Group purchased by Sanken Electric Co., Ltd., of Japan in late 1990. At the time revenues were stagnant and profitability minimal at best. Success took time, but unlike Penn Central or probably any other potential US acquirer, Sanken has proved to be a patient owner, and each successive CEO—Dick Morrison, then Allan Kimball, and today Dennis Fitzgerald—has contributed to today's success. The highly competitive worldwide automotive market accounts for more than two-thirds of Allegro's revenues. As just one example, a luxury automobile may contain

---

12 Denis Zogbi, "Vishay-Israel: Plant Tours: 1999—High Tech in the Promised Land," *Passive Component Industry* Magazine, August 1999.

more than ninety magnetic sensor, motor driver, and regulator integrated circuits, all manufactured by Allegro. As a wholly owned subsidiary, no public financial figures are made available, but in a late 2012 exchange of correspondence with the author, Fitzgerald summarized Allegro's business position as follows: "Current annual revenue is approximately $450 million, gross margins generally exceed 40 percent, and operating margins 15 percent, we have no debt and, in fact, we have been paying Sanken dividends. Allegro's operating performance continues to be ranked in the upper second quartile of analog companies." With operations around the world, the headquarters remains in Worcester, Massachusetts; led by Fitzgerald, seven of the nine top managers all joined Sprague Electric in the 1980s or before. Management stability of this kind is unheard of in the semiconductor industry.

If so many former Sprague Electric business units exist today as successful parts of other corporations or private companies, why did the original parent company fail and disappear as a single entity? It is easy to finger Penn Central as the culprit. However, the seeds of its demise were laid years before when Sprague Electric was first acquired by General Cable and ceased to be in charge of its own destiny.

Three primary causes led to this acquisition. First, the long, tortuous, and expensive process of becoming a successful niche supplier of semiconductor devices sapped the company of too much of its financial, managerial, and technical resources at a time when it could least afford it, as foreign competition, especially from Japan, intensified. While Allegro has proved that the company could have succeeded in semiconductors, this was only after an agonizing series of false starts and strategic errors. Secondly, because of the vast concentration of resources in semiconductors, Sprague Electric was never able to create a viable position in multi-layer ceramic capacitors, even as a niche supplier. Finally, the increasingly acrimonious labor relations in North Adams that led to the devastating ten-week 1970 strike nearly destroyed the company, causing major losses both financially and in capacitor market share and making Sprague Electric an excellent acquisition candidate only a few years later.

With Sprague Electric gone, just how does the worldwide capacitor industry look today? According to Paumanok Publications, in 2008 the $18 billion global capacitor market was dominated by Japanese corporations or their subsidiaries: Murata with a 12 percent market share, Kyocera/AVX at 8 percent, TDK & Nippon Chemicon at 7 percent each, Nichicon at 6 percent, and Taiyo Yuden at 5 percent. With the exception of the $2.59 billion tantalum capacitor segment, for which Kemet shares the lead with AVX at 12 percent each, this dominance is due to strength in ceramic capacitors, which in 2007 accounted for 87 percent of the more than one trillion capacitor units shipped and nearly 44 percent of the dollars. The nearly $4 billion aluminum electrolytic market, which Sprague Electric also dominated at one time, is almost completely Japanese, while the $1.6 billion AC film market is highly fragmented[13].

Ceramics, and in particular MLCCs, dominate because their technology continues to create components that can replace applications previously served by other dielectric families at a fraction of the cost. It is a tough, highly competitive market and, except for high-value specialty niches, it seems impossible that anyone can survive in a business in which the average price for the entire mix of ceramic capacitor products is less than a penny

---

13   Passive Component Market Outlook, 2008–2013 (Cary, NC: Paumanok Publications, Inc., 2008).

a unit ($0.0069 in 2007). Yet there remain a number of successful US capacitor suppliers, including Vishay with a broad mix of both passive and active devices, US-based Kyocera/AVX in ceramics and tantalums, Kemet in tantalums, and a host of smaller specialty firms. Given a chance, Sprague Technologies might have succeeded as a tantalum capacitor and networks supplier if Penn Central hadn't pulled the plug. Still, this is wishful thinking; Carl Lindner never wanted to be in that type of business in the first place.

As the Sprague era comes to a close, it is time to return to North Adams where, in the late 1980s, 87 Marshall Street was about to undergo a very different New Beginning.

CHAPTER SEVEN

FROM THE ASHES

MASS MoCA AND THE FUTURE OF NORTH ADAMS

Like all New England "mill towns," North Adams expanded through an influx of immigrants, with the population surging to fuel the growth of Arnold Print Works in the late 1800s and early 1900s. According to the 1875 Massachusetts census, they mostly came from England, Ireland, Scotland, Wales, Canada, and Germany,[1] while the Italians began to arrive toward the end of the century. While Ellis Island was the premier port of entry for most Europeans who entered the United States, full of hope for a better life, Boston also became a major immigration port. Many of the new arrivals joined the growing New England textile industry, undeterred by the long hours and harsh conditions.

As Arnold's fortunes began to wane, Sprague Specialties arrived in 1929 to find an excellent labor force ready to fill its factories. However, when Sprague departed North Adams in the 1980s and the city desperately searched for a replacement, there was none in sight. After nearly one hundred years of primarily depending on a single dominant employer, the city and its residents embarked on an alternate course that is undergoing ongoing adjustments, with the North Adams population declining steadily from a peak of 24,200 in 1900 to a low of 13,689 in 2011.

---

1   Carol Robare, *North Adams in 1875*, (North Adams Historical Society).

In the beautiful book *MASS MoCA: From Mill to Museum*, there is a statement that to this day represents the popular view that when Sprague Electric moved its headquarters to Lexington in 1985 the Marshall Street complex closed, "leaving 4,000 unemployed and North Adams 'deindustrialized' like so many cities in the Northeast."[2] Yet, the actual job loss was 550, and even in 1987 some 640 Sprague employees remained, although by the mid-1990s these would all be gone.[3]

Even if its headquarters had remained in North Adams, the company would have had to leave Marshall Street, since reduced usage had created a facility that was too large and expensive to maintain. Perhaps whoever took over the buildings would have either torn them down or left them to rot, a huge eyesore near the center of a city that already had a gaping downtown hole resulting from a late 1960s urban redevelopment project. Thankfully, along came MASS MoCA to keep North Adams securely on the map.

THE MASSACHUSETTS MUSEUM
OF CONTEMPORARY ART (MASS MoCA)

—

A visit by Thomas Krens to the Schaffhausen Museum near Zurich, Switzerland, once a textile factory and now a contemporary art museum, was one of the early inspirations for MASS MoCA,

2   Nicholas Whitman, Simeon Bruner, Joseph Thompson, *MASS MoCA: From Mill to Museum* (teNeues Publishing Company, 2000), p. 11.

3   In 1987, Wet & Foil Tantalums and Filters, the last manufacturing units still at 87 Marshall Street, were moved to two new buildings in North Adams's Hardman Industrial Park, Springfield Sunday Republican, January 25, 1987.

as was the use of non-conventional space for art installations at the documenta art fair in Kassel, Germany.[4] In 1987 Krens, the charismatic and driven director of the Williams College Museum of Art (WCMA), had with his small staff been considering several abandoned North Adams mills to use as additional space for WCMA's ambitious exhibition program. Schaffhausen suggested an intriguing possibility. Could a North Adams mill be used to house the type of massive contemporary art installations for which, at the time, little appropriate space existed in the United States?

As Krens's team began to evaluate the various alternatives, encouraged by North Adams officials—especially Mayor John Barrett—87 Marshall Street became the leading candidate. Basically identical to the property purchased by Sprague in 1944, the sprawling complex offered nearly one million square feet of potential museum and economic development space—an almost unimaginable opportunity. On the other hand, the facility was deteriorating rapidly, and it seemed that transforming the property into a museum might be nearly impossible. It would take overwhelming effort, grit, a never-say-die attitude, and luck to pull it off.

If Krens was the front man until early 1988, when he was named director of the Solomon R. Guggenheim Museum in New York City, it was another member of the small WCMA team who really made MASS MoCA happen. Tall, lanky Oklahoma native Joseph C. Thompson graduated from Williams College in 1981, receiving an MA from the University of Pennsylvania four years later and an MBA from Wharton in 1987. Thompson worked

---

4   *North Adams Transcript*, June 2, 1987.

with Krens at WCMA from 1982 to 1985, and was re-hired by Williams College to help draft the MASS MoCA Master Plan, feasibility study, and economic impact projections. When Krens left for the Guggenheim, just as the Commonwealth awarded North Adams the initial funding for MASS MoCA, Thompson was named director of the project's executive planning group, becoming founding director of the institution as it took shape. A year later, he was joined at MASS MoCA by author Jennifer Trainer, who was hired as director of development, and they soon became an inseparable team. They sealed their partnership when they married in 1991, and continue to be the heart and soul of the museum.

As the project began to take shape, Williams College played a key role. Led by president Francis Oakley and vice president for administration Will Reed, the college fronted the initial cost of developing the concept and early fundraising plans, and even pro-vided some modest early bridge financing, although Oakley had assured a nervous Williams board of trustees that no actual funds would be provided by the College.[5] A strong patron of the arts (he served as chairman of the board of the spectacular Sterling and Francine Clark Art Institute in Williamstown from 1998 un-til 2005), Oakley envisioned multiple artistic and economic ad-vantages resulting from the addition of a third leg to the existing WCMA and Clark museums. Today these three institutions are close partners, and the Clark has recently leased space at MASS MoCA for future Clark galleries and back-of-house operations.

The initial concept envisioned was vast, with an estimated cost of $72 million. In addition to mammoth museum galleries, there

---

5   *Berkshire Eagle*, June 2, 1987.

would be a conference center, restaurant, small hotel, additional commercial and industrial space, and even a river walk (à la San Antonio). More than six hundred new jobs would be created, some $21 million would be poured into the economy annually, and local and state tax revenues would increase by more than $1 million a year. Massachusetts Governor Michael Dukakis was a strong early proponent, since North Adams had yet to participate in the surging "Massachusetts Miracle" economic growth period of the late 1980s.

Besides finding art to fill the vast complex, there were still a few other "minor" details to be addressed: detailed plans had still to be drawn for the transformation of 87 Marshall Street from a decaying industrial complex into "the world's largest contemporary art museum," and except for early temporary funding by Williams College to pay the salaries of Thompson and the rest of the embryonic MASS MoCA team, there were no funds. The property remained under Penn Central ownership, and problems with toxic contamination of the site from its industrial past had yet to be addressed.

Although MASS MoCA was still only a concept in 1987, aggressive promotion by Krens, Thompson, Barrett, Oakley, local attorney John DeRosa, and a host of others quickly created a media storm, first locally, then throughout the Berkshires and Massachusetts, and finally worldwide. Reviews ran the gamut, from ecstatic (led by the North Adams Transcript), to measured (most of the outside art world), to highly negative (generally from parochial points of view). For example, Pittsfield's The Berkshire Eagle lamented the waste (while charging that the money should actually be spent for a project in South County, as opposed to North County, where North Adams is located), and in Boston there was concern that the inclusion of funding for MASS MoCA could sink the entire $100 million "Convention Bill," which was filed in July 1987.

In early January 1988, following a battle royal between Senate President Billy Bulger (whose only interest was covering the Hynes Convention Center deficit) and House Leader George Keverian (who supported broader use of the funds), the state legislature killed the entire bill and apparently MASS MoCA's future as well. However, Governor Michael Dukakis came to the rescue. Supported by Keverian, the governor filed a separate $35 million appropriation for the first phase of MASS MoCA, which was approved by the legislature in March 1988. The museum was back in business, at least for the moment.[6] In late April, a high-level board, called the Massachusetts Museum of Contemporary Art Cultural Development Commission, was appointed to oversee the project with "distinguished members of the art world," as well as Krens (chairman), Oakley, and Barrett. Joe Thompson was named executive director of the executive planning group, but soon took over management of the entire project. The Commission's first action was to approve a $1.75 million feasibility study. Following stiff competition from some thirty world-class architectural firms, in October 1988 a distinguished team of architects— including Skidmore, Owings and Merrill, Frank Gehry, Robert Venturi, and Simeon Bruner of Cambridge-based Bruner/Cott & Associates—was chosen to prepare the study.[7] From this group, Bruner/Cott emerged to create the final architectural design, which was completed in 1995.

However, MASS MoCA's future was once more in doubt as the

---

6 *Berkshire Eagle*, January 6, 1988.

7 *North Adams Transcript*, September 9, 1998.

US economy began to deteriorate, and Dukakis lost his battle for the US presidency.

The museum remained purely an intellectual exercise as the cold wind and snow of the winter of 1989 blew through the shuddering complex at 87 Marshall Street; the Commonwealth's economy began to falter, and the release of state funding dragged. Still, Thompson and his tiny team pressed on, patching together the environmental impact reports, traffic studies, and site engineering. Recognizing that local funds would be necessary to break the financial log jam, a "Founding Friends" fundraising group was formed in January 1989, and part of the facility was spruced up enough to hold a "Warehouse Ball" in mid-February. Many of the one thousand attendees were former Sprague Electric employees, who found it almost impossible to conceive how massive pieces of contemporary art could fit into spaces where they had once manufactured capacitor sections for consumer and industrial applications around the world.

By the end of 1989, MASS MoCA's debt load was approaching $300,000, with no relief in sight. Funding bills were passed at the state level, but no money actually reached the Berkshires. In the meantime, the staff survived on the generosity of Williams College and local contributions. As the fall 1990 elections approached, William Weld (who became Governor-elect in November) made it clear that he wasn't committed to either MASS MoCA or the other northern Berkshires financial hot button—Greylock Glen.[8]

Just before Dukakis left office at the end of December 1990,

---

8 *Berkshire Eagle*, September 10, 1990.

there was a flurry of activity: MASS MoCA received a $688,000 state grant (which Weld immediately revoked upon taking office); the MASS MoCA Development Commission approved a revised plan reducing the scope of the museum and the necessary funds from $75 million to $46 million (which still required $33 million from the Commonwealth); and Krens resigned from the Commission (he was replaced as chairman by Meyer Frucher). In order to convince Governor Weld that the project had area support, a group of local business leaders set a spring fundraising goal of $500,000. By June 1991, more than $1 million had been raised and a new goal set at $2.5 million.[9] As a result, Weld finally released part of the $688,000 planning funds in mid-October. But in order to gain subsequent access to the needed $33 million fund, the state required MASS MoCA to find a museum director (ignoring the fact that they already had one in Joe Thompson), secure art, and raise more private funding. Throughout his governorship (1991 to 1997), Weld successfully used a carrot-and-stick approach in releasing state funds to the museum, and the MASS MoCA staff repeatedly responded to the challenge in kind.[10] Now, with some money in the bank, talk began to be replaced by action.

In December 1993, funding responsibility shifted to a new entity, the MASS MoCA Foundation, with four general institutional and several limited partners, and the museum's mission was gradually repositioned from "the world's largest contemporary art museum" to one in which the museum would become an international, multidisciplinary cultural center, incorporating dance,

---

9 *North Adams Transcript*, April 26, 1991.

10 Joe Thompson and Jennifer Trainer, interviewed by the author,
    August 1, 2011.

music, theater, history, education, and technology, in addition
to contemporary art.[11] To a large degree, that is the institution
that exists today. The museum/center was to be constructed in
stages at an estimated cost of $18.4 million for stage one, with
nearly $13 million of this still to come from the state. The private
funding goal was given a major boost when Penn Central agreed
in early 1994 to donate the 87 Marshall Street complex (the title
didn't actually pass until August 1995), an in-kind gift credited at
$3.1 million. Penn Central also agreed to complete the hazardous
waste clean-ups and to contribute $300,000 to MASS MoCA's
contingency fund to help cover early operating deficits.[12]

In April 1995, Governor Weld and his Lieutenant Governor, Paul
Cellucci, presented MASS MoCA with a check for $600,000,
marking the first release of actual construction funds.[13] In a recent interview, Joe Thompson said that the state had contributed
a total of approximately $20 million prior to the museum's 1999
opening. The remainder of the $35 million grant from 1987 was
gradually drawn down, so that by 2006 the funds were fully in-
vested, mostly to create space for commercial rent-paying tenants.
In the process, the usable space had increased to nearly 350,000
square feet from the 1999 "grand opening" footprint of 220,000.

As Bruner/Cott & Associates rushed to complete the final detailed plans for the new museum, potential commercial tenants
began to sign intent-to-lease agreements. Groundbreaking didn't
start until later in April, but by September 24, 1995, the Night
Shift Café was able to open in Building 13's makeshift space,

---

11 *North Adams Transcript*, December 2, 1993.

12 *Berkshire Eagle*, December 7, 1993.

13 *Berkshire Eagle*, July 12, 1996.

where The Band played before fourteen hundred enthusiastic music lovers. Kleiser-Walczak Construction Company, "one of Hollywood's leading creators of computer-generated imagery and special effects," moved into the Marshall Street complex in November 1995, initially occupying 8,000 square feet. Thus, before there was any new construction, art galleries, or even art, MASS MoCA began to receive income from real estate development and music concerts, two leading and ongoing revenue generators.

Additional financial support came from multiple sources, including an October 1997 Kresge Foundation $600,000 challenge grant;[14] an $8 million Founders Fund Campaign announced in early 1998 by MASS MoCA trustee and co-chairman of the campaign Francis Oakley;[15] and a gift in the spring of 1999 from the Hunter family to fund the Hunter Center, a black box theater that is MASS MoCA's principal performing arts space.[16]

SILICON VILLAGE

—

Following a flurry of "technology" start-ups, by 1999 the northern Berkshires had earned the questionable moniker of "Silicon Village,"[17] with Williams College serving as the incubator. It started in 1992 when two classmates, Bo Peabody and Brett Hershey, joined their Williams College economics professor, Richard Sabot, in forming Tripod, an early online social net-

---

14 *North Adams Transcript*, October 7, 1997.

15 *The Advocate*, February 4, 1998.

16 *North Adams Transcript*, March 12, 1999.

17 *Berkshire Eagle*, August 11, 1999.

work that offered advice to students for a fee. Successful beyond anyone's original expectations, in 1998 it was bought by Lycos for approximately $58 million and, except for the three founders, its forty-odd Williamstown-based employees were soon moved to Lycos's offices in Waltham, Massachusetts, or terminated.[18]

Then in January 1997, Berkshire Capital Investors (BCI) was formed in Williamstown with Williams College alumni George Kennedy, Taylor Briggs, and Robert McGill as founding partners.[19] Creation of a number of start-ups followed, some located on MASS MoCA's campus and others in downtown North Adams and Williamstown. BCI was the financial catalyst for many, as was its affiliate, Village Ventures, co-founded in 1999 by Bo Peabody and Matt Harris. As the recession of the late 2000s deepened, the pace of new company start-ups in the northern Berkshires slowed dramatically; in recent years neither company has made new capital investments in the area,[20] and in early 2012 Village Ventures announced that it was closing its Williamstown operation.[21] In the meantime, MASS MoCA has continued to diversify its commercial rentals, looking for more stability than can be offered by a volatile mix of technology start-ups.

MASS MoCA OPENS

—

On Saturday, May 29, 1999, more than twelve hundred guests

18 Bo Peabody, interviewed by the author, August 30, 2011.

19 Berkshire Eagle, January 31, 1997.

20 Russ Howard (BCI managing director) to the author, November 16, 2011.

21 Berkshire Daily, February 16, 2012.

attended a lavish black-tie gala in the museum's largest gallery in Building 5. Surrounded by Robert Rauschenberg's *The 1/4 Mile or 2 Furlong Piece*, which covered 270 linear feet of wall space, they were wined, dined, and entertained into the early morning hours. The following day, thousands more visited, including many former Sprague Electric employees; with financial woes forgotten for the moment, 87 Marshall Street was once more alive with lights, music, people, and, above all, hope for the future. While the adults enjoyed the artwork and marveled at the transformation of the buildings, their children enjoyed Kidspace, created in collaboration with the Clark Art Institute and the Williams College Museum of Art. This important teaching program, located in Building 10, offers an active environment in which students, their families, and teachers can both learn about and create art. [22]Every North Adams elementary school student visits Kidspace and is taught a related in-classroom curriculum at least twice per year. Between the May 1999 opening and January 2000, more than ninety thousand visitors explored the museum, and North Adams seemed on its way back from near oblivion.[23]

There were other local signs of recovery. In late March 2000, nine mill houses across River Street from MASS MoCA were purchased by Jack Wadsworth, then a Williams College trustee and investment banker with Morgan Stanley, to be transformed into a high-end inn and run by the Fitzpatricks of Stockbridge's Red Lion Inn.[24] Named simply Porches, the inn opened for business in July 2001. In April 2000, Wynton Marsalis played in MASS MoCA's Hunter Center, the first of many sold-out concerts by

22   Berkshire Eagle, April 7, 1999.

23   Berkshire Eagle, January 17, 2000.

24   Berkshire Eagle, March 21, 2000.

outstanding artists. In August 2000, MASS MoCA received a $5.2 million federal grant for a second phase of expansion,[25] and in January 2001 Storey Publishing, LLC (founded in 1983) consolidated its operations from Pownal (Vermont), Williamstown, and Blackinton in new offices at MASS MoCA with ninety employees.[26]

Nevertheless, a year later Joe Thompson cautioned, "MASS MoCA is still financially fragile, with no endowment and no cash reserves, so we are totally dependent on earned income, the gate, and philanthropy."[27] In a March 2004 edition of North Adams's *The Advocate*, author, poet, composer and photographer Joe Manning, who has had a love affair with North Adams since his first visit in the late 1990s, issued a sober warning: "The so-called tourist economy has not panned out as predicted."[28] So by 2005, although MASS MoCA was well established and gradually moving toward financial stability, its long-term impact on the local economy remained tenuous.

Despite these uncertainties, a study by the Center for Creative Community Development, or C3D, painted an encouraging picture of what had already been accomplished. Founded in May 2004, C3D is the brainchild of Williams College economics professor Stephen Sheppard, who wanted to study the long-term economic impact of cultural institutions, such as MASS MoCA, on their communities. Initially funded by a $350,000 Ford Foun-

---

25   North Adams Transcript, August 12, 2000.

26   North Adams Transcript, January 3, 2001.

27   Berkshire Eagle, October 10, 2002.

28   The Advocate, March 11, 2004.

dation grant, C3D concluded that by the summer of 2005 MASS MoCA had already provided considerable economic stimulation. As reported in The Berkshire Eagle, since 1998 the annual payroll in North Adams had increased by $24 million, there had been a net increase of forty-four new businesses and 230 new jobs, and unemployment had dropped from 18 to 5.5 percent. Property values in North Adams increased by a combined total of nearly $14 million, mostly in those properties closest to MASS MoCA, and in 2002 the museum drew more than ninety-four thousand visitors from outside North Adams. This added $14.2 million annually to the regional and local economy, not including the economic impact of the museum's commercial tenants, which Thompson estimates spun off another $6 million in annual economic impact.[29]

In October 2006, MASS MoCA struck pay dirt when it was announced that the museum would install world-renowned minimalist artist Sol LeWitt's A Wall Drawing Retrospective, on loan from the Yale University Art Gallery and other museums and collectors until at least 2033.[30] In a collaborative effort between the Yale University Art Gallery, MASS MoCA, and Williams College Museum of Art, over the next two years more than $6.5 million was raised for an endowment and the renovation of Building 7's 27,000 square feet, using an architectural design by Bruner/Cott & Associates. During the six months before the official opening on November 16, 2008, some sixty-five artists and art students drafted and painted each of the 105 LeWitt wall drawings on nearly an acre of wall space throughout the building's three stories, using detailed instructions provided by the artist. LeWitt

29   Berkshire Eagle, July 3, 2005.

30   North Adams Transcript, October 27, 2006.

died of cancer in April 2007, never seeing the completion of the masterpiece that he knew was under construction, but with this installation MASS MoCA became a truly world-class destination museum.

Even as North Adams, the United States, and the rest of the world slipped into a deepening recession in 2008, MASS MoCA's financial fortunes continued to slowly improve. By its tenth anniversary in May 2009, the museum's developed footprint had grown to 430,000 square feet, of which 120,000 were devoted to commercial development with about twenty tenants generating much-needed revenue. In a mid-2011 interview, Joe Thompson stated that with improved operating income, along with continuing strong philanthropic support, MASS MoCA had begun to generate a modest endowment. "I think we have almost turned the corner."[31] Seven months later, the endowment had reached $15 million, and operating income was close to breaking even.[32]

Besides commercial development and installations such as the Sol LeWitt work, MASS MoCA has continued to artistically develop other parts of the complex. On September 24, 2011, the museum opened one of its most creative expansions around the long dormant Sprague Electric Boiler House, The Speed Way, which sits on five acres of the museum campus south of the Hoosic River. On top of the Boiler House, Michael Oatman's All Utopias Fell has crash landed: a silver airstream trailer "spaceship" complete with solar power and shredded parachute. But the centerpiece is the building itself, in which Stephen Vitiello has created an intricate audio installation, All Those Vanished Engines. The Boiler

---

31 Thompson and Trainer interview.

32 Joe Thompson, interviewed by the author, February 9, 2012.

House is filled with recorded sounds of the building, through which is narrated a science fiction story, written by Williams College English professor Paul Park, about a super-secret acoustic material that Sprague Electric supposedly developed there during World War II.

JLS: *In an unexpected touch of irony I was enlisted to narrate the part of the elderly, deaf, and blind engineer who managed the project. Planned or not, the name, All Those Vanished Engines, seems to allude to the transition with which North Adams struggles as it moves irreversibly from an industrial to a postindustrial economy.*

LOOKING FOR THE MAGIC BULLET...

—

If MASS MoCA has "almost turned the corner," the city of North Adams still has a long way to go. While lauding what the museum has done to improve the local economy, C3D also underlined how big a task remains. In 1900, North Adams's population made it the largest city in the Berkshires and fourth largest in the state, while today it is the smallest city in Massachusetts. The annual median household income in 2000 was $10,000 lower than Berkshire County as a whole, making it the poorest in the region.[33]

MCLA remains active in supporting the arts, including organizing the art galleries that are slowly occupying downtown North Adams. The college has a new B-HIP (Berkshire Hills Internship

---

33   Kay Oehler, Stephen Sheppard, and Blair Benjamin, "Mill Town, Factory Town, Cultural Economic Engine: North Adams in Context," C3D Report, North Adams, 1.2006, p. 14.

Program) initiative in Art Administration, offers an undergraduate degree in Arts Management, and has a new $54 million Feigenbaum Center for Science and Innovation. In 2011, MCLA's then-president Mary Grant, who was active in a number of cooperative programs in North Adams and Pittsfield, envisioned a future in which North Adams became a cooperative education center, much like the five-college system in Amherst, Massachusetts.[34] Five miles west of MASS MoCA, Williams College is still trying to define a role in local job creation, with projects such as a winter study program, LACE (Liberal Arts Collaborative for Entrepreneurship).

There is continuing discussion about how to create better linkage, both physically and philosophically, between MASS MoCA and downtown North Adams. In August 2008, the city collaborated with the museum, the Northern Berkshire Community Coalition, and Scarafoni Realty to initiate a now ongoing summer program, *DownStreet Art*.[35] As visitors leave the museum, they are provided with a map listing the city's summer and early fall cultural and entertainment events; signs and arrows painted on the sidewalks encourage them to explore historic downtown North Adams.

Over the years, the leadership of North Adams has employed a variety of cooperative organizations to help run the city, such as the North Adams Partnership, formed in January 2011 with retired State Representative Dan Bosley of North Adams as CEO, and Mayor Richard Alcombright, John DeRosa, Joe Thompson, and Mary Grant as members. Their agenda is built around the

---

34 MCLA president Mary Grant, interviewed by the author, November 4, 2011.

35 Berkshire Trade & Commerce Monthly, August 2008.

use of public/private investment to more fully integrate both
MCLA and MASS MoCA into downtown North Adams. Possible initiatives include cluster housing around the museum and
MCLA, a privatized and revitalized Heritage State Park (where
historical artifacts and exhibitions bring to life the danger-filled
construction of the Hoosac Tunnel) and Windsor Mill (a historic
building offering spaces for diverse businesses, including dance
and art studios), modest renovation of the Mohawk Theater (as
both a performing arts space for MASS MoCA and teaching
facility for MCLA), a small convention or meeting center either
downtown or on the MASS MoCA campus, and a wind farm
along the Mohawk Trail ridge.[36]

Most solutions discussed so far relate to MCLA, MASS MoCA,
the arts, and tourism. Although these will remain at the core of
an improving local economy, communities such as North Adams
need jobs from other sources. Encouragingly, there are several
current local business models that fit the available skills and
resources.

Osmin ("Ozzie") Alvarez, who studied electrical engineering
at Northeastern University, has lived in North Adams since his
family moved there from Honduras when he was only two years
old. In mid-2000 he formed Boxcar Media at 106 Main Street,
with a number of divisions, including the iBerkshires.com website, employment website BerkshireJobs.com, and RacingJUNK.
com, the largest motor sports classified ad site in the world. Many
of the forty jobs are filled by MCLA graduates who are trained

---

36   North Adams Transcript, January 11, 2011. Interviews with Grant and DeRosa (December 5, 2011), and Alcombright (December 12, 2011).

in-house.[37]

In late 2002, Streetmail, a Village Ventures investment with Bo Peabody as chairman, merged with Agora Media to form Waterfront Media and moved its twenty employees from Williamstown to MASS MoCA's campus. In 2010, the name was changed to Everyday Health, which, although headquartered in New York City, has sited its customer service center in North Adams.

Malcolm Smith (Williams College '87) formed Xtend Energy in Texas in 2005. Looking to create a Northeast base of operations, he opted for the northern Berkshires because of its proximity to the major electrical grid centers in Albany, New York, and Holyoke, Massachusetts. With his local partner, utilities expert Janette Kessler, he opened for business in Williamstown in 2006, moving to North Adams and setting up shop as a MASS MoCA tenant with about sixty employees a year later.

If Silicon Village was a fleeting mirage, these businesses certainly aren't, and it seems clear that the northern Berkshires should present an ideal location for light manufacturing, IT/call centers, and publication-oriented jobs, either standard or web-based. With today's robust telecommunication systems and Internet access, it should be possible to remotely run much larger entities from the Berkshires, while enjoying a lower cost of living and superior quality of life. By 2013, MASS MoCA had developed some 110,000 square feet of commercial office space, and an impressive 85 percent is leased to twenty-four businesses, ranging from small sole-proprietor offices to the region's largest law firms.

---

37   Osmin Alvarez to the author, December 7, 2011.

North Adams isn't alone in its economic struggles. While the Massachusetts population increased by 3.1 percent between 2000 and 2010, Berkshire County's declined 2.8 percent.[38] No community was exempt. In nearby Adams the drop was 4.7 percent to only 5,515 residents. North of downtown Adams, the huge twenty-five-building textile complex of the Renfrew Manufacturing Company is long gone. Today the acreage is home to the Adams Corporate Park, with some half dozen modest buildings housing small businesses (including the author's). Nearby, the Berkshire Textile Mill (of Berkshire Hathaway fame) is now the home of luxury apartments and several small service organizations. Further south, Pittsfield has suffered a similar fate. Once dominated by General Electric, which in the 1960s employed thirteen thousand out of a total population of nearly sixty thousand, by the end of the 1970s GE was starting to reduce its presence; today there are only seven hundred equivalent jobs in Pittsfield, with a concomitant drop in population to approximately forty-four thousand residents. So far, Pittsfield's response has been to beautify downtown and concentrate on the arts and tourism to stabilize the economy. The Berkshire Museum has been renovated partially and the Colonial Theatre completely. Newly created 1Berkshire, which combines four local agencies, including the Berkshire Chamber of Commerce, has a mission of "jobs, jobs, jobs."[39]

Even Williamstown is suffering, despite its world-renowned Clark Art Institute, *Forbes* magazine number-one-ranked Williams College,[40] Williams College Museum of Art, Tony Award-winning

---

38 Local and state census records.

39 Berkshire Eagle, April 15, 2010.

40 2012 U.S. News College Guidebook.

Williamstown Theatre Festival, and a number of wealthy retired Williams alumni who lavish support on both their alma mater and the town. The population has dropped slowly but steadily from 8,424 in 2000 to 7,754 in 2010.[41] The only remnants of a once-vibrant manufacturing presence are a partially destroyed brick factory building off Cole Avenue near the Hoosic River, and the Cable Mill building on Water Street, which continues to deteriorate while funds are sought to turn it into luxury condominiums. These buildings stand as stark reminders of the fate that could have befallen 87 Marshall Street.

Unless more new jobs can be created, the cities and towns of the Berkshires will slowly transform into retirement communities with economies ever more dependent on the arts and tourism, and the population will continue its downward spiral. Yet the situation is very different around Boston, home to some of the finest universities in the world and an increasing number of incubator centers or clusters. A recent *Boston Globe* article[42] described how these new centers have been created to help rejuvenate struggling Massachusetts cities such as Lowell and Fall River. It also noted how difficult it is to create such centers outside of greater Boston. Quoting Tim Rowe, founder of the Cambridge Innovation Center, "Cheap office space and the lower cost of living promoted by regions (such as the Berkshires) outside of Boston are not enough to spawn a cluster. Entrepreneurs want to be around other entrepreneurs, and they often want to be close to universities." Village Ventures co-founder Bo Peabody disagrees and avidly supports the idea of MASS MoCA as a "super custom-

---

41   US Census Records.

42   Scott Kirsner, "Tough going for start-up clusters outside of Boston," Boston Globe, October 2, 2011.

er service" location.[43]

North Adams will never again be an "Arnold Town" or "Sprague Town" (terms coined by Stephen Sheppard to describe periods when one company or institution dominated the local economy[44]), and "MASS MoCA Town" is not enough. There are good jobs in the arts, in education, and in tourism, but clearly more are needed. As Allen Jezouit, the owner of Williamstown-based Berkshire Direct, said in a recent exchange with Paula Consolini, the director of the Center for Learning in Action at Williams College, "We need jobs—manufacturing jobs or IT/call center jobs or publication/content creation jobs."[45]

For a community to survive, it takes not only strong, effective leadership, but also desire, will, and commitment by its citizens. The continuing success and growth of both MASS MoCA and MCLA are vital for North Adams, as is success in many of the initiatives planned by the North Adams Partnership. Perhaps the only way to tap the potential is for the city to consider hiring a full-time representative to spend one to two years in the Boston and/or New York City metropolitan areas, canvassing the business community for candidates to relocate back-office/customer service-type operations to the Berkshires.

Good people do good work. In the Preface, the question was raised: How did world-class innovators such as Arnold Print Works, Sprague Electric Company, and MASS MoCA come to be located in this seemingly remote part of the Berkshires? Quality

---

43   Peabody interview.

44   Stephen Sheppard, interviewed by the author, October 31, 2011.

45   Allen Jezouit to Paula Consolini, November 17, 2011.

of life was a key factor, but it was extraordinary individuals and leaders who made it happen. The Arnold family and Albert C. Houghton arrived in the northern Berkshires like frontiersmen, seeking a new life in a beautiful area that was just beginning to industrialize. Houghton proved to be a brilliant businessman and by 1900 had built Arnold Print Works into the finest of its kind in the world. When Sprague Specialties moved to North Adams in 1929, it was a young but established technology company in search of manufacturing space and a strong labor force. The city offered both, and because R.C. Sprague was such a remarkable engineer and manager—and fell in love with the Berkshires— he was able to build Sprague Electric into a world leader in the all-important and chaotic world of electronic components. Finally, Joe Thompson undoubtedly had no idea what he would end up accomplishing when he joined the staff at the Williams College Museum of Art. Yet when the opportunity was there to create the improbable, under nearly impossible conditions, he seized it, and where Arnold and Sprague once prospered, now MASS MoCA is there for all to enjoy.

Groups and organizations can plan how to solve the economic problems that we face today, but only leaders such as Albert Houghton, R.C. Sprague, and Joe Thompson can make it happen. Leaders are human and fallible and can and will make mistakes, but will never fail for lack of trying. The members of the North Adams Partnership and the entrepreneurs who have brought their embryonic businesses to the city seem ready and willing to lead North Adams in new directions. The northern Berkshires need more such leaders, and perhaps the burning questions are: Where will they be found? How will they be enticed to move to North Adams—and persuaded to stay? How will leaders already in the local community be nurtured?

JOHN L. SPRAGUE: *As this chronicle of the long and storied existence of 87 Marshall Street reaches the present day, I would like to share some very personal thoughts about what it has meant to be a member of the Sprague family and a witness to so many of the transformations that these premises and North Adams have experienced over the years.*

EPILOGUE
THE PERSONAL REFLECTIONS
OF A SPRAGUE IN NORTH ADAMS

JLS: *Writing this book has forced me to give deep consideration to North Adams, and my role in its history when I was an executive of Sprague Electric Company. North Adams has a remarkable record as the home of such global enterprises as the Hunter Machine Company, Arnold Print Works, Sprague Electric, and—in a totally different field—today's MASS MoCA. This durability is a testament to North Adams's many good qualities, which include a beautiful physical setting and residents who are resilient, smart, hard-working, and loyal. However, it seems clear that North Adams will never again be the home of such large manufacturing enterprises, or a one-company town, as it was with Arnold and then Sprague—a fate shared with all too many old New England factory towns.*

In hindsight, it is easy to believe that these changes to the local and regional economy were inevitable and that manufacturing was bound to leave North Adams eventually. However, this does not take away the pain of the loss, nor can we dismiss the mistakes made along the way by Sprague Electric, as well as others in the community. During my years in Sprague man-

*agement, I was forced to make tough decisions during difficult
company transformations, including the movement of jobs out
of North Adams. So looking back has caused me to try to ob-
jectively analyze what happened, and what could and should
have been done differently—if anything.*

*As recounted in Chapter Five, I never intended to work for
Sprague Electric. I wanted to make my own way in the world,
without relying on my father's help. When I joined the Navy
in 1952, what I wanted most in life was to become a naval
aviator and fly jets off carriers. Thanks to my brother, Bob, I
was already a licensed pilot, and after a year of sea duty I was
accepted for flight training at Pensacola. However, eventually I
bowed to family pressure and enrolled in the Navy's electronics
school where, as it turned out, I began my semiconductor education. Even today, I occasionally wonder what life would have
been like if I had pursued the first path.*

*When I left for Stanford University in the fall of 1955 to earn
my PhD in chemistry, my father and I drove across the country
together. Not since my childhood had we spent such a long time
in each other's company, and many warm and colorful imag-
es remain, such as his criticism that I was a lousy tipper (we
bought dinner on alternate evenings) and my refusal one night
to accompany him to a local midwest bar after dinner "for
a little dancing." (He returned to our motel room very late,
smelling of perfume, and happily humming some tune he had
picked up from the orchestra.)*

*It soon became clear that my father's real reason for making
the trip was to try to convince me to work for Sprague Electric
after graduation. I loved, admired, and revered him, so I was
flattered by his request, but I made no commitment for several*

reasons. First, I was worried that I would always be measured as a son of the founder, rather than for what I did or did not accomplish. Secondly, sensing the tension that existed between my father and his younger brother, Julian, as they worked and, in a way, competed in the same company, I could envision this happening between Bob and me.

In graduate school, by pure chance—or was it fate?—my thesis professor was performing early research in semiconductor materials, and my PhD thesis ended up being on semiconductor devices. In 1952, Sprague Electric had already begun a major research effort into semiconductors, and shortly before I graduated, my father raised the ante and made his offer even more attractive, stressing just how important my semiconductor background would now be to the future of the company.

Despite this, I applied to a number of eminent northern California semiconductor start-ups, but once they learned of my relationship to Sprague Electric none would hire me; they believed I would eventually return to Sprague in possession of their trade secrets. Yet, as it turned out, by far the most exciting opportunity was to work for solid-state genius Kurt Lehovec in the Sprague research labs, so despite my concerns I moved back to the Berkshires in the spring of 1959 and began my career in North Adams.

The half-dozen years I spent in research and development in the city were some of the happiest of my life. The work was initially interesting and eventually critical to the company's future in semiconductors. However, when I became head of the Sprague Semiconductor Group, it was headquartered in Worcester. I tried the two-hour commute for a while, but that didn't work, and Jid and I finally moved our family to the

Worcester area.

An industrial city in central Massachusetts, Worcester lacks the physical beauty of the Berkshires. Still, it proved to be a warm and friendly place, and the move worked out well for us in many different ways. Our children quickly made friends, and Jid increased her involvement in Girls Clubs of America, eventually rising to the national presidency. I was able to build an extraordinary team, with many key members transferring from the North Adams research center. The turnaround job of creating a successful integrated circuit business is one of the world's most exciting, stimulating, and difficult challenges. Yet while the future of Sprague Electric seemed to be dependent upon our success or failure, in the Worcester community the Sprague name meant nothing more than that I was head of a new business in town. I relished the relative anonymity.

While I was in Worcester, trouble was brewing at Sprague in North Adams, culminating in the strike of 1970. Sprague Electric's relationship with labor has always been controversial, even within my own family. During a recent discussion of the strike and labor issues, my oldest son, John, said in a somewhat accusatory tone, "Dad, you seem to be anti-union." Several people have, in writing about Sprague Electric, said the same thing about the entire Sprague management group. The truth is that we were, but the reality of what that means is much more nuanced than it sounds.

We certainly recognized the importance of employing an intelligent, hard-working, and motivated workforce. Sprague Electric created many jobs: at our peak we employed more than four thousand people in North Adams alone and over twelve thousand worldwide. We tried our best to create a friendly, family-like atmosphere, and to offer competitive pay and benefit packages. We were anti-union because we felt that we were doing a good job in creating a positive place to work and in having a good relationship with our workers. We felt that unions created an adversarial relationship that was not good for either the company or the employees.

There is no question that, for more than a century and within numerous industries (including early textiles), unions and collective bargaining have been responsible for the vast and much-needed improvement in working conditions and benefits for the American worker. And no doubt this continues today in some industries. However, based on my Sprague Electric experience, I do not believe that unions have benefited labor in the electronics industry.

Specifically, the Sprague strike of 1970 couldn't have come at a worse time from a business standpoint. With a recession and overcapacity in the industry, if Sprague couldn't meet its delivery schedules because of the strike, customers could easily go elsewhere unless the vendor was the sole source. Therefore, Sprague was forced to move manufacturing to other locations as rapidly as possible, and even then lost a great deal of business and market share, especially in the core capacitor segment. Also, as discussed in Chapter Five, the national union's demands were heavily based on comparing pay and benefit packages of Sprague workers with those at General Electric in nearby Pittsfield. GE made primarily large items, where the cost of labor was a relatively low percentage of total product cost; Sprague, on the other hand, made mostly small components which, in some of the capacitor lines, sold for a penny apiece or even less. The cost of labor was a large percentage of the total cost of these products, and profit margins were extremely tight. The proper comparison was not with GE, but rather between Sprague and its competitors in the electronic component industry, where Sprague offered some of the highest pay and benefit packages.

If unions really expect to serve their membership, they must also consider the state of the economy and the financial realities of the companies whose employees they represent. How does it help if union demands cause serious damage to the business, resulting in the loss of many jobs? Indeed, the strike of 1970 nearly destroyed Sprague Electric, forcing almost two thousand jobs out of North Adams. It is, in my opinion, one of the main reasons Sprague Electric no longer exists today.

Considering all this, why didn't Sprague settle with the unions sooner? Management felt that it could not afford to meet the union's demands and still remain competitive in its industry. After the settlement, those workers who remained in North Adams certainly had improved pay and benefits, but this left the company at a competitive disadvantage, which only led to the further loss of jobs later on. While Sprague was able to gradually recover, and in fact there was a period of prosperity ahead, mainly resulting from several periods of broad national economic growth, it was unfortunate that North Adams received little benefit from these good years.

With the loss of manufacturing jobs all over New England, it was probably inevitable that it would also happen to Sprague Electric and North Adams. Even so, the strike and its fallout were a particularly unhappy chapter in the history of both the company and the city, the scars of which remain raw forty years later.

When I was working in North Adams in the early to mid-1960s, I experienced no problems with the non-affiliated local unions. Worcester never had a union, and since I was working there in 1970 I did not experience the strike firsthand and never had to cross the North Adams picket lines. I knew that it was devastating to members of management, especially my father, and I know that deep bitterness still remained on both sides when I returned to North Adams as president at the end of 1976.

While Worcester was becoming successful in the mid-1970s, there was a major battle brewing between my father and the independent outside directors about the future leadership of the company. For years my father had wanted me to eventually lead the company, and in October 1976 he proposed that I be named president, a move opposed by essentially all the outside directors and a number of insiders as well. To this day, I have never been certain that I really wanted the job. I did feel I was the most qualified executive within the company, but I also wanted others beside my father to believe so. In addition, it meant another upheaval for my family, more turmoil within the company, and leaving what I was most comfortable with— the Sprague Semiconductor Group. However, as detailed in Chapter Six, the acquisition of Sprague by General Cable left no choice.

It was a bittersweet experience for me to return to North Adams as the president of the $200 million high-technology company that bore my family name. On the one hand, Jid and I were going home to an area we loved, and I had received both a great honor and an even greater challenge. Financially, the company was about to enjoy six years of growth and prosperity. On the other hand, North Adams was depressed by the after-

math of the strike and by the continuing loss of jobs to other parts of an increasingly decentralized company. While Neal Welch and I were an effective team, we were never close, and my "power base," if you can call it that, remained in Worcester. Although my father was no longer involved in the business, I was still the son of the founder, and everything I did or did not do was measured against him. Even succeeding Welch as CEO in 1980 did little to change this.

When 1984 arrived, and our new owner, Penn Central Corporation, dictated the move of Sprague headquarters to the Boston area, our North Adams employment had already dipped to below fifteen hundred. Still, the further loss of five hundred fifty jobs, larger than originally forecast, was devastating to the community.

Local officials felt betrayed, and newly elected mayor John Barrett called me a liar. For years I never understood this accusation, because I had not consciously intended to mislead the city. However, after looking back over the chronology of events, I can now understand his point of view. Our strategic planning in early 1984 did not envision such large job losses, and when we met with city officials, we told them that. Ten months later, when we announced that a much higher number of jobs would be eliminated, it hit the city hard, and the residents had every reason to feel deceived.

While I don't believe that the loss of Sprague jobs in North Adams could have been prevented in the long run, I know we could have handled the process a lot better. Decentralization, which I supported, was a continuing process that began in the 1960s and by the mid-1980s was irreversible. This was on top of the relentless economic pressure to move jobs to areas where labor costs were cheaper, especially as Asian competitors were becoming increasingly competent. As a result, we ended up creating an image of Sprague Electric as a cruel, heartless company that abandoned and cared nothing for the city that helped make it great. If nothing else, I hope that this book will, in at least some small way, change that impression.

In trying to answer questions concerning Sprague Electric's apparent lack of loyalty to its North Adams employees, I was once quoted as saying that "no one is owed a job." While I believe in the importance of being able to offer employment to others, and also in the crucial value of good relations between management and labor, I do not believe that this means one can jeopardize the survival of one's company to protect specific jobs in specific locations. Certainly North Adams was enormously important to Sprague's history, and that importance deserved major consideration. Nonetheless, the company's survival came first. Sprague moved out of North Adams because its new Penn Central owners, in dialogue with Sprague management, concluded that the company could not successfully continue its business there. The costs had become too high, the atmosphere in the city too hostile, and the location was no longer suited to our business.

However, we didn't communicate these reasons effectively. We failed to develop a constructive dialogue with the city, or explore other options for the future. Even if Sprague had to move eventually, in hindsight I should have argued for a more gradual process instead of the rapid and very expensive move to Lexington. And in the largest business mistake of my career, I should not have endorsed the highly unrealistic and disastrous goals set by Penn Central for the Actions for Profitable Growth program. I might have been unsuccessful, but perhaps the tran-

sition could have been slowed down and made less painful.

By 1987, I was effectively removed from any management responsibility, and in my largely honorary position as vice chairman of Sprague Technologies, I could only watch from the sidelines as the successor company made a brave attempt at survival, failed, and then disappeared completely as an entity. History has shown that many of Sprague's successors have thrived, and I personally believe that, given a chance, Sprague Technologies could have continued as a niche supplier of capacitors—concentrating on the tantalum dielectric system—and possibly the increasingly effective Sprague Semiconductor Group could have been retained. Yet, since Carl Lindner had no interest in such options, the possibility for Sprague's survival no longer existed, as Penn Central moved on to become an insurance company.

In concluding these personal reflections, I want to make one final observation. I believe that, since the demise of Sprague Electric, Penn Central has been a more responsible corporate citizen in North Adams than most people realize. It continued the much-needed toxic waste clean-up of the empty Sprague facilities and adjacent properties. It donated the 87 Marshall Street facility to MASS MoCA, and also underwrote some of the early museum start-up costs. Without these actions, today there would probably be no MASS MoCA to bring new life to one of North Adams's most historic sites.

APPENDIX I

SPRAGUE ELECTRIC FINANCIAL TABLES

Table 1: Sales and Profit (1941–1966)
(From Sprague Annual Reports, data in millions of $)

Year	Sales	Profit	Employees
1941	4.8M	0.21M	-
1942	7.4M	0.21M	-
1943	14.5M	0.55M	-
1944	20.8M	0.87M	-
1945	16.7M	0.65M	-
1946	10.8M	0.72M	2,600
1947	10.5M	0.66M	2,100
1948	12.6M	0.83M	2,500
1949	15.3M	1.21M	3,000
1950	28.6M	3.35M	4,700
1951	38.3M	2.66M	5,100
1952	43.4M	2.86M	5,900
1953	46.8M	2.89M	5,500
1954	42.4M	3.33M	5,000
1955	44.4M	3.00M	6,000
1956	44.7M	2.18M	5,700
1957	46.2M	2.22M	5,500
1958	43.2M	1.76M	4,900

Table 2: Sales and Profit (1966–1976)
(From Sprague Annual Reports, data in millions of $)

Year	Sales	Profit	Overhead Expenses[1]	Employees[2]
1958	43.2M	1.76M	-	4,900
1959	56.4M	3.50M	-	5,900
1960	64.5M	4.09M	-	6,400
1961	77.3M	6.09M	-	7,200
1962	87.0M	6.43M	-	8,200
1963	83.3M	4.63M	-	7,600
1964	85.7M	3.60M	-	8,100
1965	107.1M	4.98M	-	10,200
1966	141.5M	8.71M	25.68M	12,500
1967	127.4M	3.33M	29.33M	12,300
1968	132.8M	(2.83)M	29.46M	12,100
1969	147.1M	1.46M	30.13M	12,300
1970	127.5M	(6.88)M	29.78M	10,900
1971	117.9M	(8.10)M	27.12M	9,700
1972	146.7M	(0.30)M	26.69M	10,600
1973	197.7M	11.63M	32.38M	12,600
1974	214.8M	10.16M	34.36M	12,900
1975	161.9M	(10.30)M	34.15M	9,500
1976	199.6M	6.85M	36.62M	9,700

1   SG&A (Sales, General, and Administration) plus RD&E

2   Domestic employment through 1964 and worldwide thereafter

Table 3: Sprague Electric Financial Performance, (1981–1987)
(Source: Penn Central Corporation Annual Reports)

Year	Sales	Profit	Overhead Expenses
1981	438M	54.3 M	-
1982	405M	40.2M	-
1983	428M	33.7M	66.5M
1984	571M	40.2M	83.5M
1985	492M	(44.2)M[3]	88.0M
1986	449M	(160.2)M[4]	86.8M
1987	437M	6.5M	78.4M

Table 4: Sprague Technologies, Inc.
Financial Performance
(Source: STI Annual Reports)

Year	Sales	Profit	Comments
1987	437M	3.6M	Discontinue MLCCs
1988	505M	13.2M	Recession begins second half
1989	344M	(98.2)M[5]	$40M IBM shortfall
1990	315M	(49.3)M	SellSemis&Fil-Mag;closeMLCC'sfor good
1991-92	294M	(52.5)M	Linder CEO; sell or close everything else

---

3   Includes $33 million in restructuring costs (plant closings and consolidations)

4   Includes $136.6 million reserve for asset redeployment

5   Includes $79.7 million restructuring reserve

APPENDIX II

SPRAGUE ELECTRIC PLANAR PROCESS TIMELINE

When	Who	Where	What
1925	J. Lilienfeld	USA	CuS solid state amplifier
WWII	Many	Worldwide	germanium (Ge) & silicon (Si) for radar detectors
1945	M. Kelly	BTL	Solid State Research Lab
Dec. 1947	J. Bardeen & W. Brattain	BTL	Ge point-contact transistor
Jan. 1948	W. Shockley	BTL	Junction transistor
1948	J. Little & G. Teal	BTL	PN junction in single crystal GE
1953		Philco	Electrochemical transistor
1955	W. Shockley	Shockley Semi. Lab	Photoresist patterning & SiO_2 masking
1955	J. Atalla	RCA	Planar PN diode
1958	R. Noyce & G. Moore	Shockley Semi. Lab	Led "traitorous 8" to Fairchild Semiconductor
1958		Fairchild	NPN & PNP MESA transistors
1958	J. Kilby	TI	Semiconductor integrated circuit
1959	H. Loar	BTL	Si epitaxial transistor
1959	J. Hoemi	Fairchild	Si Planar NPN transistor
1959	K. Lehovec	Sprague	PN junction isolation patent
1961		Fairchild	Micrologic IC family
1961-1963		Sprague	Silicon epitaxial planar transistor (SEPT) and IC (UNICIRCUIT)

APPENDIX III

ROBERT C. SPRAGUE AND NUCLEAR DETERRENCE

"Due to its complexity I was involved in the study [of the Russian nuclear first-strike capability against the US using intercontinental bombers] for nearly seven months, from September 1953 until March 1954, twelve to fourteen hours a day, seven days a week. Initially I met with Admiral Arthur Radford, chairman of the Joint Chiefs of Staff, and the heads of the services themselves, and then key government and military officers as I traveled around the country."

    – ROBERT C. SPRAGUE
      interviewed by his grandson, David Sprague, 1985

The sensitivity of the information R.C. was sharing with David had pretty much disappeared with the airing of the 1987 PBS documentary, *The Nuclear Age*, in which R.C. was interviewed, and the publication of its companion book, *War and Peace in the*

Nuclear Age.[1] One of the most startling revelations concerns a November 1953 exchange R.C. had with General Curtis LeMay during a briefing at the Strategic Air Command (SAC) headquarters in Omaha, Nebraska. They were in a room with some fifty of LeMay's staff when R.C. asked a question concerning potential target cities in the USSR, to which LeMay replied, "Mr. Sprague, your question concerns war plans which I will not answer nor would I answer if it were from the president of the United States instead of from you—for all I know I may have a couple of Communist spies in the room!" It seems that LeMay already had SAC aircraft flying over Russia and was prepared to make an immediate preemptive strike if it appeared the Russians were planning an attack. When R.C. commented that this certainly wasn't national policy, LeMay stated, "No, but it is my policy!"

In early January 1954, R.C. felt he had all the information he needed and began a series of presentations of his findings and conclusions, first with Admiral Radford and senior officers of all the armed services, and then the Senate Armed Services Subcommittee, which prepared a top-secret report for President Eisenhower. Now recognized as the person in the United States, and probably the world, most knowledgeable about "Continental Defense," R.C. was appointed by the president as a consultant to the National Security Council, a position he held from May 1954 through December 1957. He also served on the steering committee of the so-called Killian Committee,[2] which was formed in the fall of 1954 and comprised fifty-eight distinguished scientists and

---

1 John Newhouse, War and Peace in the Nuclear Age (New York: Alfred A. Knopf, 1989).

2 Named for its chairman, Dr. James R. Killian, president of MIT, and Special Assistant for Science and Technology (or Presidential Science Advisor) to Eisenhower from 1957 to 1959.

engineers. While its role was to continue and expand the studies already underway on Continental Defense, it did so primarily from the point of view of intelligence and the security of communications in time of war. Based on a suggestion by one of its members, Dr. Edwin Land of Polaroid, one of its most important contributions was the development of the U-2 spy plane. This flew over Russia at prodigious altitudes for four years, until Gary Powers was shot down by a Russian missile. It was also responsible for formation of the SAGE Air Defense System and the MITRE Corporation; R.C. served on the board of trustees of the latter for many years, chairing it for two.

The most important advisory group that was formed during this period of extraordinary tension between the United States and Russia was the Security Resource Panel, better known as the Gaither Committee after its initial chairman, H. Rowan Gaither Jr.[3] It was launched in April 1957 and was the largest civilian committee of its kind ever established, comprising ninety-one distinguished individuals with broad and varied experience on military and economic matters, and a staff of more than twenty. As defined by Eisenhower, its mission was to analyze and make recommendations concerning the nation's position relative to Russia in active and passive defense. R.C. was named co-director and took over as director when Gaither was stricken with cancer in September 1957. With a ten-member steering committee, advisory panel, subcommittees, project managers, executive staff, and administrative and secretarial staff, management of the entity was more than a full-time responsibility. Yet it seems that R.C.

---

3   Rowan Gaither was a distinguished California lawyer, who had served as Business Manager for the MIT Laboratory for Electronics during World War II (it developed military radars toward the end of the war), and currently was chairman of both the Rand Corporation and Ford Foundation.

was up to the task.

The final report was given to the National Security Council[4] on November 7, 1957, and was sobering, controversial, and debated to this day. The report's recommendations included greatly improved protection of US strategic assets, both military and civilian; expansion of the nuclear ballistic arsenal; increased capability to wage limited military operations (more than fifty years later, still a major priority); a reorganized Defense Department; and a major civilian fallout shelter program. The estimated cost of the program was more than $44 billion, to be spread out over four to five years. Excluding fallout shelters and limited war capability, Eisenhower apparently agreed with the bulk of the report, although subsequent presidents, including John F. Kennedy, had different reactions.

---

4   There were nearly seventy attendees, including President Eisenhower; Secretary of State John Foster Dulles; Secretary of Defense Neil McElroy (who succeeded Charles Wilson), and Secretary of the Air Force James H. Douglas (Harold Talbott had resigned in 1955). Apparently, like today, the terms of presidential appointees were often short!

ACKNOWLEDGMENTS

Throughout the research stage, my assistant, Jean Lee, offered invaluable assistance, particularly in tracing articles relating to the history of Sprague Electric in local newspapers such as the North Adams Transcript and Berkshire Eagle. Similarly, Fred Windover, who worked for me as chief legal officer in the latter days of Sprague Electric, was an early reader of the manuscript, providing critical input on copyright issues, and has been a key interface in helping to obtain needed information from Penn Central. His wife, Joan Windover, provided the wonderful 1947 Anniversary Album that was the main information source for the section in Chapter Two on the James Hunter Machine Company.

John Storey, founder of Storey Publishing, read an early draft and provided useful feedback. This was also true of William D. Middleton III, co-author with his father of the Indiana Press biography of my grandfather, Frank Julian Sprague, published in 2009. Bill gave strong positive support as a peer reviewer and helped format this manuscript.

Williams College president emeritus and good friend Francis Oakley has provided encouragement and support, as well as an excellent Foreword. His daughter, Deirdre Ann Oakley, associate professor of sociology at Georgia State, not only provided further encouragement, but also noted many of the sociological issues surrounding the job losses in North Adams.

Williams College has been an important resource throughout. Geology professor Reinhard ("Bud") Wobus provided much of the geological history used in Chapter One, while history professor Robert Dalzell referred me to Williams College senior honors theses by Carin Cole and Anthony Parise that provided little-known and important historical background, especially related to the industrialization of North Adams and the Arnold Print Works. Robert Volz and Wayne Hammond of the Williams College Chapin Library, along with archivist Sylvia K. Brown, not only made these theses available for study, but also recommended other sources of information. Finally, a 2012 Williams College honors thesis by Alison Pincus about Sprague Electric, The Mark of Reliability, made me realize how much local bitterness and misinformation related to Sprague Electric's mid-1980s departure from North Adams still remains. This led to my interview with former North Adams mayor John Barrett, and some changes and expansion of the manuscript including, indirectly, the Epilogue.

MCLA has been another important historical resource. Linda Kaufman and Susan Denault at the MCLA Freel Library identified and made available such sources as W. F. Spear's 1885 History of North Adams and Timothy Coogan's excellent NYU PhD thesis. While retired professor Maynard Seider and I have often clashed philosophically on labor relations issues, he provided valuable information about Sprague Electric that he had obtained from the Penn Central archives, as well as an incomplete manuscript he is currently writing. We remain friends.

Another resource has been the North Adams Historical Society (NAHS), which contains a wealth of information on the history of the northern Berkshires. Here Lorraine Maloney, some years ago, and now Charles Cahoon and Gene Carlson, have been invaluable resources; many of the early photos used in this history came from their voluminous files. The NAHS deserves far more support than it receives locally.

I also want to thank Denis Zogbi and Paumanok Publications, Inc. for allowing me to use selective data from Passive Component Market Outlook, 2008–2013. Now that the Electronics Industry Association no longer exists, Paumanok is the only source of such information.

Probably the most interesting sources of information have been personal interviews, either by telephone or, wherever possible, person-to-person. Especially in the case of former Sprague employees and associates, it has also been a way of renewing old friendships, if even fleetingly. With one unnamed exception, everyone has been open and glad to talk. From Sprague Electric, Don McGuiness, Bill O'Connor, Pete Loconto, Dick Morrison, Bob Milewski, and especially Dennis Fitzgerald (president of Allegro Microsystems) corrected my memory and filled in missing gaps as we reminisced about the (sometimes) "good old days." I spoke on the phone with former Sprague Technologies CEO Ed Kosnik and lunched with "Pug" Winokur, my last boss at Penn Central. Pug provided a view of Sprague Electric from the Penn Central side, which was both informative and sobering.

Local movers and shakers, including former mayor John Barrett, current mayor Richard Alcombright, John DeRosa, and former MCLA president Mary Grant, have provided their views on a revitalized North Adams with an economy based primarily on the arts, tourism, and education, while local business heads and entrepreneurs Pam Art, Bo Peabody, Matt Harris, Bob McGill, Russ Howard, Osmin Alvarez, Malcolm Smith, and Patrick Brennan provided direct experience and ideas on different business models to complement the arts and tourism. From Williams College and C3D, Stephen Sheppard provided detailed analysis on what MASS MoCA has contributed to the North Adams economy and what still needs to be done. Blair Benjamin of MASS MoCA did the same, describing a detailed initiative to bring more "back-office" jobs to North Adams. Jim Hunter added to the James Hunter Machine history, while Pittsfield Chamber of Commerce CEO Michael Supranowicz and Williamstown business owner Allen Jezouit have simultaneously called for more "jobs, jobs, jobs"!

Local historians Joe Manning and Paul Marino have offered their own thoughts on the past and future of the northern Berkshires. And finally I must thank Paulette Wein and Jane Calverley, whose exhaustive review and attention to detail has brought this manuscript to where it is today.

Everyone previously cited has made important, and sometimes critical, contributions to this manuscript. However, more than anyone else, my oldest son, John, and my co-publisher, Joe Thompson, have had the greatest influence.

Mired down and needing fresh input, in the spring of 2012 I asked John to be my editor. An Amherst College English major with an MA in Comparative Religion from Vermont College, John immediately began to attack discrepancies in structure, grammar, and format. Even more importantly, he challenged the objectivity of some of my views on labor relations and North Adams job losses, and the resulting debate was educational and important for both of us. Like Bill Middleton before him, he urged me to personalize more of the text, which led to additional memories of my own Sprague Electric experience and ultimately to the Epilogue. His input has helped create a far superior manuscript and in the process made us closer as father and son.

With so much local history and an almost immediate market potential, publication of 87 Marshall Street by MASS MoCA Publications seemed a logical next step. But when I first spoke with museum director Joe Thompson he tried to discourage me, as did his wife, Jennifer Trainer, herself an accomplished author. They cited the process as too long and difficult, said most such books fail completely financially, and—politely unsaid—wondered if I really could write. A sample chapter fascinated both of them, and reluctance gradually changed to enthusiasm as I continued to forward the rest of the manuscript. Finally, a simple handshake between Joe and me sealed the bargain. He is an extraordinary and talented individual and manager, with more irons in the fire than seem humanly possible. While at times this has slowed the process, here we now are. Simply put, without Joe's support there would be no 87 Marshall Street for many years to come, if at all, and I wouldn't be writing these acknowledgments!

John L. Sprague
Williamstown, MA